ESSENTIAL
VOLVO 120 SERIES
AND P1800

E S S E N T I A L
Volvo 120 Series
AND P1800

T H E C A R S A N D T H E I R S T O R Y 1 9 5 6 - 7 3
A N D E R S D I T L E V C L A U S A G E R

Published 1996 by Bay View Books Ltd
The Red House, 25-26 Bridgeland Street,
Bideford, Devon EX39 2PZ

© Copyright 1996 by Bay View Books Ltd
Edited by Mark Hughes
Typesetting and design by Chris Fayers & Sarah Ward

ISBN 1 870979 74 5
Printed in Hong Kong

CONTENTS

A SCANDINAVIAN SAGA

It is rather odd how the image of a make of car can vary substantially from market to market. Volvo is a classic example. In its Swedish homeland – and in Scandinavia generally – a Volvo is a workhorse, the stand-by of the police forces and the darling of the cab rank. The estate car or even the van derivative is the preferred choice for small and not-so-small businesses, advertising respectability and modest prosperity. To the private buyer, the solid Scandinavian citizen, a Volvo is a natural step on the ladder of automotive aspiration, on a middle rung somewhere above Volkswagen or Opel but below Mercedes-Benz. Those few Scandinavians who find a Volvo too boring or conformist can always opt for the still-safe alternative of the slightly more eccentric and

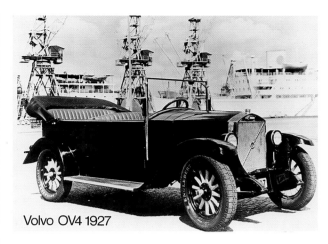

Volvo OV4 1927

Four generations of Volvo cars from the company's own museum collection (left), from ancestor Jakob, through the Carioca and PV544, to an early example of the 120 series Amazon. Founding fathers: Assar Gabrielsson and Gustaf Larson (top) in the early post-war period, when both were still active in the company. The first production Volvo (top right) – the ÖV4 or 'Jakob' touring car of 1927. The original Volvo factory (above), a former SKF plant at Lundby in Gothenburg, still the only assembly plant until the 1960s.

racier Saab, which some might describe as the thinking man's Volvo…

In the USA and Canada, Volvos are appreciated for rather different reasons, to do with their undoubted durability, reliability and safety, the fact that they are built for cold climates, and also because they are perhaps the imported cars most closely attuned to North American tastes, with styling and appointments that often echo Detroit themes. The Volvo is reminiscent of the sort of robust and sensible car the Americans like to think they used to make, the ultimate reincarnation of the Ford Model A, and thus becomes equally acceptable to the New England academic, the mid-western farmer or the style-conscious Californian computer buff.

In Britain, a Volvo has become a status symbol. In the Thatcherite 1980s, a Volvo estate car became a lifestyle accessory for suburban yuppiedom, the world of green wellies and golden labradors. It was the perfect second car, provided you already had a Porsche. It was ideal for those trips to Ikea to collect a pine futon base and perhaps some gravad lax. The fact that Volvo styling was unattractive – often described unflatteringly as tank-like – was almost a point in its favour with a sector of society that also elevated the Barbour jacket to high fashion.

Things began to change in the 1990s. Volvo caught up with prevailing trends in car design and brought out the front-wheel drive 850 model, which was praised for quite different reasons compared with the previous Volvo generation. Here was a Volvo of somewhat sporting demeanour and with performance enough, in turbocharged form, to make an impression on the race tracks. Figures such as 0-60mph in little more than 6sec and a top speed of over 150mph were bandied about. Yet the estate version was still sufficiently four-square and load-lugging not to frighten the traditional Volvo clientèle away, and overall the image of high quality, longevity and safety remained untarnished.

In Britain at least, the present-day Volvo image dates largely from the introduction of the 140 series in 1966. Those car enthusiasts of the 1990s who are only slowly beginning to admit that some Volvos, at least, appeal to them, may be surprised to learn that 30 or 40 years ago

Somewhere in Sweden (left), an early PV444 meets a surviving PV4 fabric-bodied saloon, some 20 years its senior. By 1929, Volvo had progressed to a six-cylinder engine, first fitted to the very American looking PV651 (below).

Volvo's reputation in the UK – and, to a degree, in North America – was built on the make's success in, of all things, motor sport, and Volvos were thought of primarily as sports saloons – to the British a kind of modern Riley without the burden of a heritage.

One can only speculate that the early British reaction to the Amazon, which went on sale in the UK in October 1958, must have greatly puzzled the marketing people back at base in Gothenburg, but they were quick to exploit the situation – and, of course, a Volvo had won the 1958 European Rally Championship. Only when Volvo pulled out of motor sport in 1966, and as their new models became less sporting, did the image begin to change. Even so traces of sporting ancestry lingered on into the early 1970s, with the last 1800s still around as a reminder of the glories of yesteryear.

By the time Volvos were introduced to the major export markets of Europe and North America, the marque had already reached maturity. The first Volvo car had been made in 1927 and it had long since been a household name in Scandinavia where, as late as 1960, 65 per cent of Volvo car production was sold. If you think that Sweden is an unlikely place to set up car manufacture, think again. Apart from her interminable forests, Sweden possesses a variety of natural resources, including substantial deposits of iron ore, which were becoming increasingly exploited for the manufacture of goods ranging from sheet steel to ball bearings as the 19th century gave way to the 20th. A few one-off cars were built in the 1890s, the best-known of the early Swedish cars being the Vabis with roots going back to 1897, and the Scania from 1902 onwards. These concerns later merged and, in 1924, decided to concentrate on the commercial vehicles which are still made to this day. In the 1920s, the promising Thulin was made in small numbers but was unable to compete against much cheaper imported American cars.

The Volvo company was originally an off-shoot of the famous Swedish ball bearing manufacturer, SKF, which had in fact already registered the trademark 'Volvo' (Latin for 'I roll' or 'I rotate') in 1915 and for a few years sold certain types of bearings under this name. The concept of the Volvo car was born at a meeting

The inspiration for the PV36 Carioca (right) was clearly the Chrysler Airflow, also imitated by other European car makers such as Fiat and Peugeot. The final descendant of Volvo's pre-war line was this 800-series (below) which survived in small-scale production until 1958.

widespread practice in the USA and also used to good effect by Morris in Britain. Volvo engines came from Pentaverken (later a Volvo subsidiary), chassis frames from the armaments manufacturer Bofors, and soon Svenska Stålpressnings AB at Olofström (the name means the Swedish Pressed Steel Company) became the leading body supplier until they were taken over in 1969. Many components, however, were imported, chiefly from the USA or Germany, as there were no Swedish sources.

between SKF's sales manager, the economist Assar Gabrielsson (1891-1962), and the engineer Gustaf Larson (1887-1968). Over a famous crayfish lunch in 1924, they agreed to co-operate on the creation of an all-Swedish car. Larson, who had experience in the British motor industry, undertook the design, while Gabrielsson concerned himself with raising the capital for the venture. He succeeded in convincing the SKF board of the merit of the project. Thus SKF re-launched their subsidiary company, AB Volvo, with Gabrielsson becoming managing director on 1 January 1927. They turned one of their existing factories in Gothenburg over to car production: the Lundby plant on Hisingen island was to be Volvo's home for the next 35 years.

From the start it was proposed to build the Volvo as an assembled car, but the philosophy which became known as 'the Volvo way of building cars' ('Bygga bil på Volvo vis') was actually hardly revolutionary, as it was

Larson's design was for a conventional touring car, with a four-cylinder side-valve engine just short of 2 litres, developing a modest 28bhp. The chassis had a generous wheelbase of 2850mm (about 112in), but originally only rear-wheel brakes were fitted. The first type, the ÖV4, had a four/five-seater open touring body designed by Swedish artist Helmer Mas-Olle. This model later became known as the 'Jakob' – a piece of Volvo folklore has it that the first prototype was completed on 25 July 1926, on what in the Swedish calendar is Jacob's day. While the prototypes mostly had disc wheels, the production cars which began to emerge in 1927 featured American-style wood-spoke wheels with detachable rims. From the start, the badge adopted for Volvo cars was the symbol for iron, the circle with a diagonal arrow that is also used to denote the male gender.

Larson and Gabrielsson are among the dignitaries looking over Volvo's new baby, the first PV444 at the show in Stockholm in 1944 (top).

The original PV444 dashboard (above), with central instruments – right-hand drive was not offered. Colours were ivory and green!

Only 996 of these early four-cylinder Volvos were made up to 1929. The open tourer had soon been supplemented by a saloon model, the PV4, PV standing for *personvagn* or passenger car. The chassis also formed the basis for the first Volvo lorry. Commercial vehicle production would soon assume great importance for the young company – only in the late 1940s did annual car production exceed that of trucks. While the first Volvo cars were clearly inspired by contemporary American models, this became even more evident in 1929 when the first six-cylinder car was introduced. All subsequent pre-war Volvos had side-valve sixes, starting out at 3 litres, later increased progressively in size to 3670cc and 90bhp. The final versions of this design were made as late as 1958, although post-war versions were almost exclusively supplied as taxis or ambulances.

As private cars, Volvos became established in Sweden in the 1930s, competing chiefly against medium-priced American imports. Hardly any Volvo cars were at this time exported, nor did the company as yet have any thoughts of entering the small car market which in Sweden was dominated by German imports such as Opel

A 1955 model of the PV444, sporting a new radiator grille. This was **the first year for the large one-piece rear window.**

and DKW. The best pre-war year was 1939 with total car production of 2834 – comparable at best to one of the smaller British specialist car makers such as MG but well behind Rover or Jaguar.

The design of Volvo cars throughout the 1930s continued to follow American themes; Ivan Örnberg, chief engineer from 1931 until his death in 1936, had worked for Hupmobile in the USA. His most remarkable design was the PV36 Carioca of 1935, the first Volvo with independent front suspension and with an all-steel saloon body inspired by the Chrysler Airflow. Being expensive, the Carioca was not a great success commercially as only 500 were sold, but its body styling allied to a more conservative front end survived on the PV51 to PV56 models which continued in production even into the early years of the war. These cars reverted to the beam front axle and were up to one third cheaper than the Carioca.

But Volvos were still not cars for the masses. While ideas for a smaller car had been considered already in 1938-40, when Olle Schjolin designed his PV40 with a rear-mounted 1.6-litre two-stroke engine, with eight cylinders in X-formation and a Roots blower, this project was soon abandoned. Volvo began during World War II to look forward to a post-war period when it was expected that Sweden's traditional supply of small cars from Germany would be non-existent. Similar thoughts were behind the design of the first Saab car, which was based on the DKW. The design of the smaller post-war Volvo was inspired by Helmer Petterson, who was hired as a consultant in 1943. His ideas were executed by a team of Volvo engineers led by Erik Jern. At first Petterson and Jern considered a front-wheel drive car, but it was decided to stick with rear-wheel drive.

The new car was designed over a period of less than 18 months in 1943-44. As was usual with Volvo, it incorporated many features typical of American cars. The body styling, with a rounded fastback rear end, had similarities to the 1941 US Ford, although another source of inspiration was the German 1939 Hanomag 1.3-litre

Gunnar Engellau became Volvo's boss in 1956. Here he proudly shows off the 50,000th PV bound for the USA. An additional model was the PV445 estate car, also called the Duett. This is a 1957 model, one of the last with the split windscreen.

model, one example of which was closely studied by Volvo's engineers. In terms of construction, the new Volvo followed the Hanomag's example of adopting unitary body and chassis, and the size and packaging were also like the German car.

The all-new four-cylinder engine, with overhead valves for the first time on a Volvo car, displaced 1414cc and originally developed a modest 40bhp; many features of its design resembled the Fiat 508C 1100 engine. The suspension featured coil springs all round, independent at the front with double wishbones, while the live rear axle was located by a Panhard rod and diagonal torque arms. Originally many components of American manufacture were incorporated, such as a Carter carburettor, a Spicer rear axle and Wagner brakes with Lockheed hydraulics.

The new car, the PV444, was introduced to the Swedish public as early as September 1944 at a special Volvo exhibition in Stockholm, where it was launched with a provisional price of 4800 Swedish kroner (then less than £300). Tagged as 'the Swedish beauty', the car aroused enormous interest and Volvo took no fewer than 2300 firm orders at the original price without quoting a delivery date! In Britain, the PV444 was described in detail in *The Motor* in January 1945 and attracted praise for its modern appearance, practical features and expected above-average performance.

Although further public display of the prototypes went hand in hand with extensive testing during 1945-46, it was not until February 1947 that the first

production PV444 cars came off the Volvo assembly line. By then the home market price had increased to Skr 6050, although Assar Gabrielsson insisted that the original orders should be met at the provisional price. Demand was such that the first production run, scheduled at 12,000 cars, was sold out by March 1947, and contracts for a new Volvo changed hands in Sweden at up to twice the list price of the car. Only small numbers were set aside for export: Belgium received a few cars in 1947, and the PV444 was available also in The Netherlands, Norway and Denmark by 1950. In 1951 annual car production for the first time exceeded 10,000, and in 1955, when the first Volvos were exported to the USA, more than 32,000 cars were made.

Although the PV444 was the model which set Volvo on the path to international success, there were a few minor diversions on the way. The large pre-war type six-cylinder model continued in small-scale production as the PV60, which was discontinued in private car form in

Introduced in 1958, the PV544 could be recognised by its one-piece curved windscreen. The American setting is entirely appropriate.

1950 although the face-lifted PV800 series was made mostly for taxi use for a further eight years. Volvo did consider a replacement, the outcome being the Philip prototype of 1950, the first project for Jan Wilsgaard, a 20-year-old youngster who had recently been hired as Volvo's first chief stylist. A large saloon on American lines, Philip had styling reminiscent of the Kaiser Manhattan, and was powered by a 3.6-litre V8 engine which was later used in the Volvo Express truck. Philip itself did not proceed, although the one-off prototype survives in Volvo's own museum.

The short-lived, unsuccessful P1900 sports car is discussed in chapter 4 (page 38), while details are found in chapter 2 (page 16) of the various early proposals for PV444 replacements which eventually led to the Amazon – or 120 series – of 1956. Meanwhile, Volvo had decided to invade the US market. If you believe the fictional account of Patrick Dennis, an early Volvo owner was his raffish Auntie Mame who brought an example of 'this divine little Swedish car' back to New Jersey in time for Christmas 1956. In real life, the first PV444s arrived in California in 1955 where they were touted as 'the family sports cars'. Early success in local motor racing helped to put Volvo on the map, and, in response to US demands, the company began to offer the twin carburettor engine with 70bhp in 1956 (the standard engine by then gave 51bhp). An estate car, the PV445 Duett, was available by this stage, a four-speed gearbox was offered as an alternative to the original three-speeder, and in 1958 the model was updated with, at last, a one-piece curved windscreen instead of the original split V-screen. The

split rear window had disappeared in 1955. The revised car became the PV544.

The original idea that the 120 series Amazon (see chapters 2 and 3) should replace the PV was largely forgotten in the end. The PV544 was an excellent supplement to the more modern but more expensive Amazon, the addition of which gave Volvo a two-car range, both models using the 1.6-litre engine originally intended only for the 120 series. By 1961 Volvo had a three-car range as the P1800 coupé was added (see chapters 4 and 5), and the 1.8-litre engine from this car was soon also fitted to both the saloon cars. The PV544 in fact handsomely beat the original PV444 model in terms of production and sales figures, and by the time the PV544 saloon was phased out in 1965 combined production of the two models had reached 440,000 cars. The estate car, now called the P210, continued until 1969, and the PV445 and P210 ranges of estates and commercials added a further 90,000 to the overall total.

The next new Volvo generation appeared in 1966, the first of the long-lived 140 series, which in turn gave way to the 240 series. Both had six-cylinder offspring, 164 and 264 respectively. The 140/240 models took the company into the 1980s, by which time a different breed of Volvo had appeared. In 1975, Volvo took over the car business of the Dutch DAF company, well-known for its small cars with continuously variable automatic transmission. The DAF 66 became a Volvo 66, and a new DAF-developed model – the 343 series, later the 340/360 series – was from the start launched as a Volvo.

Volvo's next step forward came in 1982 with the

Towards the end of its career, the PV544 was fitted with the B18 engine, as indicated by the red badge on the radiator grille.

launch of the 700 series, which formed the basis of the 900 series that continued in production into the 1990s. From 1984 the Dutch-built 400 series followed as the first Volvos with front-wheel drive, the eccentrically-styled 480 coupé soon being supplemented by more conventional 440/460 hatchback and saloon models.

These cars helped to pave the way for the new generation of senior Volvos made in Sweden. The 850 was the first big front-wheel drive Volvo, launched in 1991 with a unique transverse five-cylinder engine. The styling was unmistakable but it was what lay beneath the skin that created all the excitement. A generation that had not known the PV and Amazon in their heyday found it difficult to accept a Volvo that might be fun to drive.

As the 1980s became the 1990s, there were portents that the European motor industry would inevitably contract to a smaller number of larger firms, with American or Japanese multi-nationals strengthening their presence. Of Sweden's two established car makers, both hitherto firmly independent, Saab was the first to succumb, coming under the influence of General Motors. Volvo, it seemed, was destined for a similar fate and the banns were read for the wedding with Renault, a relationship that went back some 20 years to the time

By 1965 Swedish cars were well-established in Britain. At the Total test day (above), two Volvos share the billing with a Saab. The 1800 coupé carries the registration X 1800 seen on several Volvo demonstrators. Volvo's range in mid-1963 (right): three variations of the 120 series, the PV544 and the now Swedish-built 1800 coupé. Missing, however, is the PV-based P210 estate car.

when Volvo first began to co-operate with the French company in the matter of engines for their Dutch adoptees. However, at the last moment a revolt by Swedish shareholders kept Volvo independent. At the same time that Volvo was wooing (or being wooed by) Renault, the company also entered into an affair with Mitsubishi, the resulting offspring being the jointly-developed Dutch-built car which came on the market in 1995 as the Mitsubishi Carisma and Volvo S40.

Sweden also belatedly joined the European Community in 1995. The Swedish-Dutch Volvo company, however, had had a European, even international, outlook for many years. For whatever reasons, its cars occupy a unique niche in most markets, their traditional virtues having a strong appeal to a wide range of customers. And recent news from Gothenburg suggests that even more exciting cars are to come.

We are only just beginning to see the erstwhile strait-laced Mary Poppins unfurl her magic umbrella and take flight. As the cars of the 21st century seem increasingly to be the same in looks, price and performance, there is a lot to be said for any car maker which can offer something different. In Volvo's case it may be a unique blend of comfort with excitement, the snug, familiar, old blanket that turned into a magic carpet. For Volvo, life begins – or blossoms once again – at almost 70. And yet Volvo's past contains cars which in their day were just as exciting as any of the new generation appearing today…

BIRTH OF THE 120 SERIES

With the PV444 successfully established in Sweden, and also increasingly in export markets, the men in the design departments at Gothenburg turned their thoughts to new projects. As we have seen, the hastily-abandoned Philip showed that one idea was to keep a foothold in Volvo's traditional big-car market, yet understandably at the start of the 1950s this was a low priority. Far greater importance had to be attached to the eventual replacement for the PV444.

While this model was still relatively young and would indeed only achieve its greatest commercial success at the end of the decade, there was a feeling that the styling was

The 1959 Earls Court show was the third for the 120 series (previously the car had been seen in 1956 and 1958). Volvo fitted one of its show cars with a Perspex bonnet.

very much yesterday's model. But as always when you try to replace a successful product, there were difficulties, and a great many avenues to be explored. Mostly they turned out to be cul-de-sacs.

The first attempt at doing something with the PV came from outside Volvo with an idea proposed by Stockholm businessman Gösta Wennberg, who

The first proposal for a PV444 replacement was 'Elizabeth' (right), styled by Michelotti and built by Allemano. Styled in-house by Jan Wilsgaard, project P179 (below right), later named 'Margaret Rose', was another proposed PV444 replacement, conceived in 1952 and completed by 1954.

After P179 was cancelled, Helmer Petterson, the inspiration behind the PV444, submitted this suggestion for a new model (below), coded PV454. In parallel with Petterson's PV454 proposal, Wilsgaard created project 55 (bottom) – and this was to evolve towards production as the 120 series.

commissioned Italian designer Michelotti to develop a special body for the PV444. Michelotti did some sketches for the Swiss Ghia-Aigle coachbuilding company to which he was then under contract, and they showed a two-door four-seater coupé very much in the contemporary Italian manner. Wennberg obtained a chassis for a PV445, the separate-chassis commercial version of the PV444 which was normally offered with estate or van bodywork, and this was dispatched to Turin, apparently with the intention that Vignale should build a body to Michelotti's design, although Allemano ended up doing the job. The finished car was in due course presented to Volvo for inspection. It looked neat enough, with its Alfa-like radiator grille, but the rear seat was rather cramped because of the packaging limitations imposed by the use of a separate chassis.

Still it was felt that the idea was promising enough to take a stage further. While the original car – named 'Elizabeth' to tie in with the Philip prototype – was sold to a private customer, Vignale was commissioned to build a second car, this time basing it on a floorpan from a unitary construction PV444 saloon. This car, completed in 1954, was also attractive but had an over-fussy full-

This was the first Amazon brochure in English, distributed to visitors at the 1956 Earls Court show. The car was – predictably – labelled as 'a Swedish beauty'. This was the heyday of Ingrid Bergman and Anita Ekberg!

When the 120 series invaded USA (left) in 1959, the cars were typically fitted with extra bumper bars. The early interior colour schemes were also two-tone (above), often in a combination of vinyl and cloth, or all-vinyl as on this car. Rubber mats were standard on all cars.

width grille. It was roomier than its predecessor, and Wennberg entertained hopes that Volvo would agree to having a series of perhaps 200 similar cars built. When the car was costed out on the basis of having the bodywork built in Sweden, it turned out that a realistic sales price would be around Skr 20,000, so Volvo decided not to pursue Wennberg's plans.

Influencing this decision was probably also the fact that, unknown to Wennberg, Volvo had by 1954 a completed prototype for a PV444 replacement. This was prosaically known as project P179 but was later, when revealed to the press, given the name 'Margaret Rose' to perpetuate the idea that cars were named after members of the British royal family. P179 was styled by Wilsgaard, who was under instruction to retain the characteristic roof line of the PV444. Despite this apparent handicap,

The 1.6-litre cars of 1956-61 had this style of radiator grille (below), with fine background mesh and substantial transverse bars.

Well-proportioned side view (top): although this car is a 1959 model it is still typical of the early 120 series. Right-hand drive was offered from the start (above), helping to make the 120 series acceptable to British motorists. The blue sections of the seats are cloth.

the result was quite attractive. Bearing in mind that the car was styled in 1952, the front end in particular looked futuristic with its large rounded-off air intake – possibly Wilsgaard drew inspiration from certain Pininfarina bodies of the period. Experiments were made with different two-tone colour schemes, split by a side feature line similar to that used on the 1953 Studebaker, but in the end a simple contrast-colour roof was deemed

adequate. The car had full-width styling, the bold front wings with a razor-edge crease, their line running through the doors to small tail fins. The fastback roof line and the window shapes looked somewhat like the PV444, but the glass area was usefully larger. The headlamps were a prominent feature, set in large bezels in the valances between the grille and the front wings.

The P179 would have used largely PV444

mechanicals, although the suspension was redesigned and turned out to be very similar to the layout eventually used on the 120 series. However, the P179 met with a sceptical reception in some quarters, the original begetter of the PV444, Helmer Petterson, apparently not liking it. There were also concerns that it would be too heavy for the 1.4-litre engine. In the end the P179 was cancelled, and the only prototype was eventually scrapped after being damaged in a road accident.

Helmer Petterson persuaded Assar Gabrielsson that he should be allowed to submit a proposal for a new model, code-named PV454. At the same time, Gustaf Larson asked Wilsgaard and Volvo's interior stylist, Rustan Lange, to submit new proposals, known respectively as Project 55 and Project 65. Petterson's PV454 was a modernised PV444, although not as competently executed as P179. It retained the fastback roof line and also had separate rear wings, while the front end had overtones of Loewy's 1953 Studebaker with two separate nostrils for the radiator grille – perhaps this was where the 120 series grille came from? The Lange car was also a fastback, with fairly heavy lines and an impossible-looking arrangement for the rear window and quarterlights. It had an aggressive front end, with a large oval grille reminiscent of the American Cunningham sports racing car. Wilsgaard contented himself with submitting a proposal which was really little more than a modified version of the original Elizabeth designs, with yet another radiator grille.

After all three proposals had been viewed in 1953, the decision was taken that Wilsgaard should develop his Project 55 but combine it with features from Petterson's PV454. This was the sort of situation which is every stylist's nightmare, but at least the dictum that the new car must have the PV444 fastback roof was soon forgotten. Wilsgaard in fact was able to develop Project 55 more or less according to his own ideas, although at least the divided radiator grille from the Petterson car was incorporated and survived through to the eventual production version – the 120 series.

The conflict of whether the new car should replace or supplement the PV444 was finally resolved when Volvo's management decided to keep the PV444 in production and develop a new car which in terms of interior room would be more competitive with cars of the next size up, such as the Mercedes-Benz 180. This must have represented a neat challenge to Volvo's package engineers as they were also told to use the same 2600mm (102.4in) wheelbase as the older car. Incidentally, the decision to move the new car, by now known as the P1200, slightly

up-market caused some studies to be done for a new smaller car, but this got no further than a styling scale model. Wilsgaard and his team had quite a busy time of it, working on the small car, as well as developing two different proposals for the final version of the P1200. Wilsgaard's preferred design was executed in clay model form mostly in his spare time…

When the final decision was made, it turned out in favour of the spare-time design. Although all studies so far had been for two-door cars, it was agreed to go ahead with a four-door version. By late 1953 or early 1954, the design was finally signed off, and development of the production version went ahead. The car also around this time acquired its name, Amazon, from the race of female warriors of Greek legend. The individual model type numbers and the general designation of 120 series came from the P1200 project number.

Although the Amazon was going to be slightly shorter than the PV444, the new car would be wider and also heavier, by about 220lb (100kg). The old B14 engine from the PV444 was therefore bored out from 75mm to 79.37mm, which increased capacity to 1583cc. When fitted with a single Zenith carburettor, the new B16A engine gave 66bhp (the SAE rating that Volvo customarily quoted at the time). Additionally, there were plans for a Sport engine fitted with two SU carburettors in the manner of the P1900 and the PV444 Sport, this B16B engine having a substantially better output of 85bhp (SAE). The bigger engine would help to consolidate the Amazon's position up-market from the PV444, although the 1.6-litre engine had also found its way under the stubby bonnet of the PV444 by the time the Amazon was in full-scale production.

The three-speed gearbox, with synchromesh on second and top, was carried over from the PV444 complete with lengthy floor-mounted lever – by then a somewhat old-fashioned feature – and would remain in use on basic Amazons for a long time, although it was soon supplemented by an excellent fully-synchronised four-speed gearbox. This was Volvo's own 'box but was based on a German ZF design (and will, reputedly, bolt straight onto pre-war BMWs!).

The running gear largely used tried and tested PV444 features, although the front suspension with coil springs and double wishbones was modified in detail. A front anti-roll bar was standard. The rear suspension was redesigned as it had been on the P179 project. Where the PV444 had rear torque arms running diagonally in towards the centre of the car, the Amazon had twin radius arms either side, located parallel to the prop shaft.

The handbrake mounted outboard of the driver's seat was an unusual feature. The door sill treadplates stamped with the Volvo name added to the impression of overall quality.

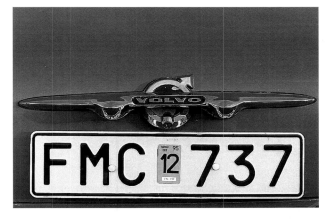

Whereas early cars had two separate boot handles and numberplate lamps, this one-piece type incorporating the Volvo name and distinctive logo came into use in 1959.

There was still a transverse Panhard rod and the Amazon rear axle was well located by any standards. The coil springs were mounted on top of the rear axle. Shock absorbers front and rear were telescopic. The cam and roller steering was similar to that of the PV444. The brakes were Lockheed hydraulic with Wagner drums, and the handbrake was unusually positioned outboard of the driver's seat. The rear axle had hypoid bevel final drive.

Wilsgaard's final styling for the Amazon was reasonably up-to-date by 1956 European standards, if a year or two behind American practice. There were some similarities to Virgil Exner's 1955 'forward look' Chryslers which also had the divided radiator grille. Some contemporary US commentators wondered whether Volvo had purchased the redundant body tooling for the '53-'55 Willys Aero! (Volvo had not – these tools were shipped off to Brazil). The Amazon luckily avoided most of those short-lived styling fads which plagued many British cars of the 1956-59 period: only the two-tone colour schemes were typical of the time, and perhaps the dashboard and interior design, but generally it was a well-proportioned and rather handsome car, with a certain timeless feel to it.

Whereas the PV444 was only ever really a four-seater, the slightly wider Amazon was at least an occasional five-seater, although rear seat access was restricted by the wheelarch intrusions which were inevitable due to the short wheelbase. The interior was well furnished, with upholstery in a two-tone combination of cloth and vinyl. Prototype pictures showed floor carpeting but all production models had serviceable rubber floor mats. The driving position was quite low in relation to the height of the dashboard and window sills, and felt sporting in a vintage manner, the driver sitting close up to the large and almost vertical steering wheel.

The dashboard layout was perhaps uninspired. Curiously, although Volvo over the years experimented with several other dashboards, production Amazons were unchanged to the end of production. A combination instrument in front of the driver was dominated by a horizontal strip speedometer, supplemented only by gauges for fuel and water temperature, trip and total mileage recorders – the latter as yet with five digits only! – and assorted idiot lights. The main dashboard was metal, painted in the body colour, but the top was padded and covered with black vinyl – one indication that Volvo was already then becoming safety-conscious – and this padding was carried over into the front door trims. The steering wheel was slightly dished, but still fitted with a large and brightly plated horn ring and plating on the two spokes. Over towards the passenger side of the dashboard was a sensibly-sized ashtray, and spaces for fitting a radio and a clock. The absence of a glovebox was often commented on by road testers but there was a flexible parcel tray on the passenger side, and also front door pockets.

From the start, the Amazon had seat belt mounting points, and Volvo's three-point lap and diagonal seat belts, invented and patented by Volvo engineer and safety expert Nils Bohlin, were offered as an option. In 1959

Under the bonnet, everything was neatly laid out and easily accessible. This is the twin-carburettor 1.6-litre engine of a 122S. Note the six-volt battery.

While the padding on top of the dashboard was an early concession to safety, the horn ring and plated spokes would now be frowned upon.

Not the roomiest of rear seats, but the folding centre armrest and grab straps on the rear of the front seats are nice touches.

they became standard equipment in most markets. The heater was standard and was of course particularly effective, being fitted with a two-speed fan. Other noteworthy equipment included two-speed wipers, a windscreen washer, a radiator blind and a headlamp flasher – all reflecting the needs of winter driving in Scandinavia.

For the same reason, rust protection was comprehensive by the standards of the period: Amazon bodies were roto-dipped in rust preventing primer and the car was finished off with bitumastic underseal. Most of the bright exterior trim was in stainless steel or anodised aluminium. An unusual feature on a European

Nighthawks, Swedish style. The original two-tone colours were **gradually replaced by monotone, which predominated by 1961.**

car at the time was that the ignition key also operated the starter. The electrical system operated on six volts only, then still acceptable in Europe and the USA if archaic by British standards, but the battery was generously rated at 85Ah, and the starter motor was a beefy 1bhp unit to ensure that it could cope in sub-zero temperatures.

Apart from seat belts, optional equipment included a radio, a clock, a brake servo and fully-reclining front seats. In 1961 a few cars with the three-speed gearbox were fitted with an automatic clutch, of a type similar to the German 'Saxomat' system. Another rarely-seen option was that the four-speed Amazon could be fitted

with a steering column gearchange and a front bench seat – this seems to have been intended to make the car more suitable for taxi use and was probably restricted to certain export markets. The only brochure mentioning this I have seen dates to 1961 and was printed in Portuguese!

This, then, was the car that Volvo was getting ready to reveal to the world in 1956: an attractive car with good performance, built to a high standard, fitted with many then unusual features. It was a car which would undoubtedly appeal to Volvo customers of old, and would likely as not also draw converts into the fold. Far more than the quirkily-styled, old-fashioned PV444, this was a car that Volvo had every hope would be seen as a worthwhile contender in the international markets. It was also expected to have a long production life, and as we shall see, it lived up to every expectation.

120 SERIES IN DETAIL

The B16-engined 122S, as launched at the Geneva Motor Show in 1958, **had twin SU carbs; power rose from 66bhp to 85bhp.**

Volvo's way of introducing the new model was a little unusual. The first official confirmation that the long-expected new Volvo was on its way was made in February 1956, and two months later a set of 'teaser' pictures was released to the press in Sweden and world-wide – in Britain they appeared in *The Autocar* for 20 April 1956. At this time there was no indication of what the car would be called, nor even of what lay under the bonnet – Swedish commentators speculated that the car might have a six-cylinder engine. The photos showed

one of the prototypes (with the Gothenburg registration mark O 52338) looking typical of the early Amazons with its two-tone paint scheme and whitewall tyres, and in most respects similar to subsequent production models except for such details as the shape of the front indicators, the absence of mesh in the radiator grilles, the presence of

Volvo letters on the rear bumper and the lack of model badging on the front wings.

If Volvo was a little coy about the detailed specification of the new car, the company was quite prepared to accept orders with a deposit of Skr 4000 against the expected price of Skr 12,500, which in the event turned out to be Skr 12,600 (£868). For comparison, in December 1957 a standard model PV444 cost Skr 9520 (£656) and a PV444 Special Skr 9995 (£689). By August 1956, Volvo confirmed that the new car would be called the Amazon, and it was also revealed that it would be fitted with the 1.6-litre four-cylinder engine. It was stated that volume production would begin in January 1957; it seems that 1956 production amounted only to 249 pilot-production cars.

The international debut of the Amazon followed at the motor shows in the autumn of 1956. At London's Earls Court in October 1956 Volvo for the first time took a stand at a British show, displaying the Amazon together with the PV444 and the soon to be discontinued P1900 plastic-bodied sports car. Although Volvo had begun to export the PV444 to the USA in 1955 and indeed had developed the P1900 with an eye to this market, the make was still largely unknown in many European markets, and in Britain the PV444 was particularly handicapped by being available only with left-hand drive. Although Sweden drove on the left until September 1967, the Swedes traditionally preferred left-hand drive cars. By contrast the Amazon was from the start offered with either left- or right-hand drive.

The early cars appear all to have been finished in two-tone colour schemes, black or red with a contrasting light grey roof, or light grey with a black roof; dark blue with a light grey roof became available in 1958. Single-colour schemes – including all black – may have been used on a few cars but only became prevalent from 1961 onwards.

The first year's production was intended to be about 5000 cars, or around ten per cent of total Volvo car production. As intended, volume production got under way in January 1957 and the first cars reached home market customers in February/March. Build-up was slow, however, and during the first nine months of 1957 only around 1600 cars were registered in Sweden (compared with 19,000 of the PV444 model). In fact it took to the end of the '1957' model year, in February 1958, to make a total of 5184 Amazons (see detailed figures on page 76). When it came to introduce the model in export markets, there was a slight hiccup when the German moped manufacturer Kreidler protested over Volvo's use of the name 'Amazon', which Kreidler had registered in most European countries. So while the Volvo remained the Amazon in Scandinavia, in other markets it became known as the 121 or, with the twin-carburettor engine, the 122S (later just 122). The range became commonly known as the 120 series.

The 122S was launched at the Geneva motor show in March 1958. Fitted with the twin SU carburettor 85bhp engine, performance was usefully improved. This was the first model to be fitted with the new all-synchro four-speed gearbox, which was subsequently fitted on most export cars, although the three-speed remained standard in Sweden. In Switzerland the 122S's price of Sfr 11,650 compared with such cars as the Borgward Isabella TS, Citroën ID19, Ford Zodiac and Sunbeam Rapier, all in the Sfr 11,600 to 12,000 bracket, while the MG Magnette ZB, perhaps the British car closest in spirit to the 122S, cost Sfr 12,950.

An early Amazon delivery in an export market occurred on 16 April 1958 when one of these cars was formally presented to HRH Princess Margrethe, heir to the Danish throne, on her 18th birthday. Now Queen Margrethe II of Denmark, she remains loyal to the marque after almost 40 years and uses a Volvo for her private motoring – although she is reputedly much less interested in cars than her late father, her husband or her two sons!

In Britain the proper debut of the 122S was at the 1958 motor show, by which time Volvo, after a tentative beginning with Victor (Swedish Vehicles) Limited of Malden in Surrey, had appointed Brooklands Motor Co Ltd, a branch of the Lex group with a Bond Street address, as its UK concessionaire. There had been no Volvos at Earls Court in 1957, but in October 1958 the 122S featured on a stand booked by the Swedish parent company, and the car went on sale at £1399 (including purchase tax). This was quite expensive for a 1.6-litre saloon when a Ford Zephyr cost only £916. Although until 1960 the Volvo still incurred import duty, the comparable (but two-door) Borgward Isabella from Germany cost only £1245.

The new car was well received by British motoring journalists. *The Autocar* had already tested a 122S provided by the Dutch Volvo importers in June 1958 and had measured a top speed of no less than 94mph (151kph), stating 'It is fair to point out that there is no other full four-seater family car of like engine size even to challenge the Amazon's performance'. As *The Autocar* was ruefully to admit in 1962 when failing to get much more out of a 1.8-litre 122S, that original 1958 road test car had been specially tuned by the makers! Indeed, *The*

VOLVO * THE 120 SERIES

The 1964 model year brochure (left) shows the wider mesh and B18 badge on the radiator grille of the B18-engined models. Early B18-engined 122S at Tower Bridge (right) has been fitted with wing mirrors and a fog lamp of British origin. Apart from the Volvo three-point seat belt, this brochure illustration (below) also shows the early fluted all-vinyl trim of the 1963-64 period.

Motor in January 1959 measured an average top speed of only 89.3mph (144kph). Even this figure was extremely good by contemporary class standards, although a good MG Magnette ZB was almost as quick at 87mph (140kph) if slower when accelerating through the gears.

This was where the Amazon's reputation as a sporting saloon came from: high performance was coupled with good, safe road-holding and handling. If the car was found to be a little firmly sprung, its behaviour on unmade roads, or in wintry conditions, was universally praised. Bill Boddy in *Motor Sport* would have preferred a remote-control gearchange as he objected to the combination of a willowy gear lever with a slightly stiff gearchange, but otherwise he liked the car very much.

In the USA, the 122S was launched at the New York motor show in April 1959, with an initial list price of $2895, and incidentally all North American 120 series cars over the years were to have the twin-carburettor engine. With the PV444 already well-known in the US, the 122S was readily accepted, although it compared unfavourably on price with the new compact cars being launched by the domestic industry. Base-model four-door sedans of the 1960 model year compacts – Chevrolet Corvair, Ford Falcon and Plymouth Valiant – were all listed at around $2000. The Volvo's excellent performance for its engine size, the make's sporting reputation and the car's much-praised safety features, as well as its impression of quality and durability, quickly

convinced many US and Canadian buyers of its merit.

Some small changes were already being made. The 1959 models sold in Sweden and in some export markets had front seat belts fitted as standard. The heater was improved, and larger self-servo brakes were fitted. The two separate boot handles were replaced by a single central fitting incorporating the Volvo symbol. American-specification cars were typically fitted with an additional tubular front bumper guard. For the 1961 model year, improved and differently styled seats were fitted, featuring centre panels in cloth with vinyl borders and offering more lateral support as well. Gearboxes were

improved, the three-speed 'box now having synchromesh on first. A Laycock de Normanville overdrive operating on second and top became available as an option on the three-speed 'box, which remained available only on the 66bhp 121 model. Also on this model, an automatic clutch was briefly available during 1961.

After 84,299 of the 1.6-litre engine four-door saloons had been made, the 120 series received the new B18 engine in August 1961. Although at first sight the dimensions of 84.14mm × 80mm suggested merely another bore increase, for a capacity of 1780cc, the engine was in fact totally redesigned with the crankshaft now running in five main bearings, and had been first seen in the P1800 coupé in 100bhp (B18B) form. There were two 120 series versions: the single-carburettor B18A with 75bhp (SAE) and the twin-carburettor B18D with 90bhp. The twin-carb model was known initially as the 122S/B18 but this was soon simplified to just 122.

The three-speed gearbox was now found only on a few home market cars and disappeared altogether in 1962. Four-speed gearboxes were the order of the day, and the overdrive option was now found only on the four-speed, twin-carb model, operating on top gear only. All models were fitted with a 12-volt electrical system. Only the twin-carb version had Girling brakes with discs at the front; the single-carb car had to wait for these until

The 1962 Earls Court motor show was the first British show for the 121 estate car. Volvo is still noted for making large load-carriers...

1964. The B18-engined models could be distinguished externally by reshaped radiator grilles with a wider mesh, and B18 badges at front and rear. Only single colour schemes were now available.

Soon after the start of the 1962 model year, Volvo brought out alternative body styles for the 120 series. First came the two-door saloon, cheaper than the four-door although at first sold only in Sweden and other Scandinavian markets where it was – rightly – considered to be yet another nail in the coffin of the PV544, although the old-timer nevertheless lived on into 1965. Available also with the choice of the single-carb or twin-carb engine, the two-door models were officially called type 131 or 132 respectively, although they were and are commonly referred to under the four-door type designations of 121 and 122.

Except for wider doors and tilting front seat backs, the two-door was in all respects just like the original four-door but had a small edge in performance thanks to its lower weight. The overdrive was not offered on the 132 two-door twin-carb model. All the early Scandinavia-only cars were black with beige trim. By mid-1962, the two-door had reached North American and other export markets, in Canada for the first time carrying the name Volvo Canadian. In Britain, however, the two-door only became available in 1964 in single-carb form, followed in 1966 by the twin-carb version.

The estate car was introduced in February 1962. This was a handsome and particularly roomy four-door model, known in Sweden as the 'herrgårdsvagn' (literally, 'manor house car'), with the type designation 221. It was at first available only with the single-carb 75bhp engine, except in North America where, as usual, the twin-carb engine was offered. In other markets the twin-carb version followed in 1965, becoming, naturally enough, the 222, although again these cars are often known simply as 121 or 122 estates. The rear axle and rear suspension were slightly different from the saloon models. A notable feature was the 6ft long load space obtainable when the rear seats were folded. There was a horizontally split two-piece tailgate, and the rear bumper overriders had rubber-faced tops so you could stand on them to load a roof rack. The overall length was about 40mm more than the saloon models.

Around the turn of the year 1961-62, the 100,000th 120 series car was manufactured. Some 1962 models, at least export versions of the 122/132, had new all-vinyl seat trim with fluted centre panels. The paint colour range was now white, slate blue, mist green, fawn and black, with ruby red reserved for the 122, while dark grey and light grey were also quoted from time to time. The 1963 models were fitted with reversing lights as standard. On 1964 models a new simplified rear number plate light housing, pioneered on the estate car, was fitted also on the saloons. Volvo now for the first time offered a fully automatic gearbox, the Borg-Warner type 35 three-speed becoming an option on four-door saloons, fitted in conjunction with the single-carb engine in Europe but with the twin-carb engine in North America. The gear selector was on the steering column.

About the time that the 1964 models went into production, on 11 September 1963 the first car came off the line at the assembly plant that Volvo had opened at Dartmouth, Nova Scotia, in Canada, this one truly qualifying for the name Volvo Canadian. From now on Canada, and also to some extent the USA, was supplied with Canadian-assembled cars. This was Volvo's first factory outside Sweden, but in 1965 another facility was opened at Ghent in Belgium.

There were to be extensive cosmetic revisions on the 1965 models. The radiator grilles had a simpler pattern with three vertical bars to each nostril and less prominent horizontal centre bars. There was a new design of pierced road wheel, with smaller hub caps in stainless steel where the central 'V' motif had a black instead of a red background. The interior was completely new, with perforated vinyl seat trim with a ladder pattern to the centre panels, and for the first time Volvo fitted the famous anatomical seats with adjustable lumbar support and stepless reclining backrests.

On the mechanical side, all cars now had front disc brakes, while the twin-carb saloon and the estate had a brake servo as standard. Volvo introduced galvanised sills on all models – an industry first. By now 120 series production had been moved to the new factory at Torslanda outside Gothenburg, the official opening ceremony having been performed by Sweden's ageing king, His Majesty Gustav Adolf VI, who was driven around the new factory in a rare surviving example of Volvo's first car, the 1927 ÖV4 or Jakob. It went almost unnoticed that the traditional radiator blind had been deleted on 1965 model 120 series cars.

On 20 October 1965 the last PV544 saloon was built, but the 210 estate car would survive until 1969. To recompense Volvo buyers for the loss of this entry-level model, Volvo introduced a bargain-basement version of the 120 series, known as the Amazon Favorit or Amazon Quick in Scandinavia, or as the 121 Standard in other markets. This was a spartan two-door single-carb saloon fitted with the old three-speed gearbox last seen in 1961. In a throwback to the days of the Ford Model T, the Favorit was available in any colour you liked as long as it was black – white was added later! – with red interior. On single-carb models a Stromberg carburettor was fitted. Twin-carb engines now had a new camshaft and gave 95bhp. Both engines had compression raised from 8.5:1 to 8.7:1. Chassis modifications included the fitting of a pressure limiting valve for the rear brakes, and front suspension and steering grease points were abolished. Saloons were fitted with radial-ply tyres. The 1965-66 model year was to be the most successful for the 120 series with total production of 119,000 cars, and the model was well established as Sweden's number one seller.

In August 1966 the new Volvo 144 four-door saloon, first of the 140 series, made its debut. This range would eventually replace the 120 series, although for the time being all the older models stayed in production and there were even a few new variations. However, production of the four-door 120 series was scaled down and in 1967 this was the first body style to be discontinued. Both engine versions had power further increased to 85bhp and 100bhp respectively. While the overdrive option on

In its native Sweden (above), the 121 estate found a ready following – for leisure activities as well as business purposes. This 1966 122S four-door (right) shows the new style radiator grille and road wheels which had been introduced for the 1965 model year.

the 122 four-door was discontinued, the availability of the automatic gearbox was extended to twin-carb saloons in Europe, as well as to two-door saloons and single-carb estate cars. Common to all models was a new grille with horizontal and vertical bars in pairs, and the rear suspension was improved with longer trailing arms. The three-speed Favorit was now sold only in Scandinavia.

The most exciting of the 1967 120 series models was the new 123 GT, which was, strictly speaking, type 133. This was a two-door saloon fitted with the 115bhp B18B engine from the 1800S coupé, offering a top speed of around 104mph (167kph). Externally it could be distinguished by wing-mounted rear view mirrors and auxiliary fog and long-range driving lamps. Inside there was a unique three-spoke steering wheel and an afterthought of a tachometer mounted on top of the

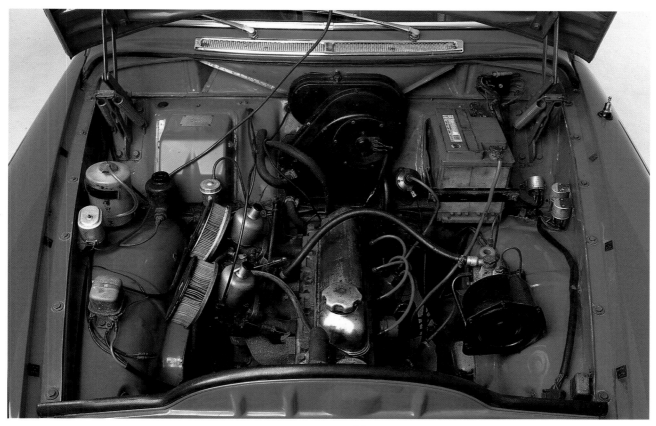

Under the bonnet of a twin-carburettor B18-engined car, now with a 12 volt system and also a brake servo. This much-revised interior (below) with ladder-pattern seat trim came with the 1965 models and lasted to the end of 120 series production.

From the rear, estate styling (with divided tailgate) was simple but still quite handsome and pleasing (right). Above all, this was a functional car as can be appreciated by looking at the cavernous interior, which has obviously seen some use!

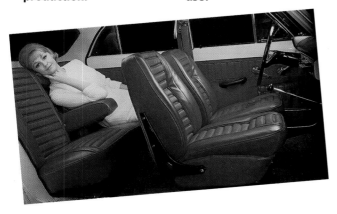

Volvo developed specially-equipped versions for Police use, such as this 122S estate which appears to be on the strength of the Gothenburg force.

The millionth Volvo, a two-door 120 series (left), was built in 1966, by which time 120 series production was well installed in the Torslanda factory.

This body production line (top right) is from the Olofström factory, at the time still an independent company: it was taken over by Volvo in 1969. Where it all came together (right) – 120 series cars nearing the end of the assembly lines at Torslanda.

dashboard. Standard colours were red, white or dark green. The 123GT was now the only model in the range fitted with overdrive, and it was the first 120 series car to have an alternator as standard. Incidentally, in South Africa, where the GT was not marketed, the 115bhp engine was offered in both four-door saloons and estates, as the 122S-B18B model.

No exact production figures seem to be available for the 123GT, but one estimate suggests that only 1500 B18-engined cars were made in the 1967 and 1968

model years. Although in some markets the 123GT label lived on into 1969, by then the car had the same engine power as other twin-carb cars and so was only distinguished by its extra equipment.

Generally speaking, 1968 model year 120 series cars were available only in two-door or estate forms. They had a new four-spoke steering wheel with the spokes in a 'flat' cross, and the steering column was collapsible. On single-carb models, the servo was now also standard equipment. On all twin-carb cars, the compression was

now 10:1 and 115bhp was quoted for all twin-carb engines – in effect the GT specification. Cars bound for North America were fitted with the first emissions control equipment as well as other features to meet new US regulations. The automatic gearbox option was withdrawn on all models.

Partly under influence from the US requirements, but also because Sweden introduced stricter construction and design regulations, several features were introduced during 1968 on 120 series cars for all markets, including dual-circuit brakes and a combined ignition/steering lock. From the start of the 1969 model year, the new B20 series engine, really a B18 bored out to 88.9mm for a capacity of 1986cc, was introduced. The output was 90bhp or 118bhp in single- or twin-carb form. Exhaust emission control was fitted for all markets, alternators were standard across the range and the cooling system was of the sealed type. As the 140 series now included an estate car, the 120 series estate was discontinued during the 1969 model year, as was incidentally the 210 estate, the last version of the 25-year-old PV design.

With the coming of the B20-engined 120 series, the three-speed Favorit had been discontinued. The 123GT lived on in some markets in name only; now fitted with the 118bhp B20 engine, only the overdrive and the

New for 1967 was not only the revised grille but this more sporting 123GT model. The driver, nevertheless, is still wearing a hat in this contemporary publicity shot! A GT it may be but above all it's still a Volvo...

More typical as a colour on the 123GT is bright red. This German-owned example has been fitted with wider wheels, a common modification.

trimmings distinguished it from a 122S saloon. Only the two two-door models were left, with 90bhp or 118bhp engines and manual four-speed gearboxes. The 1970 models were very little different, with only front seat headrests and rear seat belts being added to the standard specification, while in some markets the bumper overriders were deleted on B20-engined cars.

Annual production by now was down to just under 20,000 cars, the lowest model year figure since 1959, and on 3 July 1970 the last Amazon left the Torslanda assembly line. In some overseas factories production lasted a little longer – a report published in South Africa in November 1970 stated that the 122S 'continued in production there indefinitely as an assembled model' – but they were probably just exhausting the stock of CKD kits! Allowing for the fact that there may have been some additional production in the overseas factories after the last Swedish-built car was made, the total production figure for the 120 series cars had amounted to at least 667,323 cars over a period of almost 14 years.

Along the way there had been a few diversions worthy of mention, although none was an official Volvo

The 123GT interior (right) showed several unique features, including a three-spoke steering wheel, add-on tachometer and small shelf on top of the dashboard. The rear compartment of the 123GT (below) was the same as on all the late-model two-door cars. The 1968 model year 120 series were fitted with this four-spoke steering wheel (below right) and the steering column was of the collapsible type. The 120 series boot (bottom), here on a 123GT, offered plenty of room for luggage, while the vertical spare wheel was still easily accessible.

effort. In 1960 Danish Volvo dealer Ole Sommer had a one-off coupé built on a shortened chassis from a PV445 estate car, incorporating 120 series panels for the front end while the rear body was hand-built with aluminium panels. The car used a twin-carb B16 engine. Its windscreen was a 120 series rear screen. The seats, rear screen and other parts were taken from various Jaguars, a make for which Sommer was the Danish agent. The car was originally sold, but in 1968 it was bought back by Sommer and added to his sizeable private car museum on the outskirts of Copenhagen.

On 3 July 1970 production came to an end with this B20-engined black two-door model (left). One man's dream turned into reality: Ole Sommer's Danish interpretation of a Volvo-based coupé (below) was to remain a one-off.

Another rather special 120 series was the convertible constructed by Belgian coachbuilder Jacques Coune in Brussels. This car was introduced in 1963, and was based on the two-door saloon. Coune removed the roof structure and introduced some stiffening, with noticeably deeper sills; he amazingly also went to the trouble of re-working the rear shutline of the doors! The interior was completely re-trimmed in leather which perhaps helped to offset a price some 50 per cent above a standard saloon model. Reputedly only four of these cars were built, plus one even more special two-seater version. It is doubtful whether any of them exist to-day, although there are some latter-day private roof chops around.

In Britain the Ruddspeed-tuned Volvos attracted notice in 1964–65. Ken Rudd worked on both the 120 series saloons and estates, and also on the 1800S coupé. His first stage of tuning included a special camshaft, a polished head with a 10.5:1 compression ratio, stronger valve springs and improved manifolding for 108bhp, which translated into a 107mph (172kph) top speed. The suspension was lowered, and Koni dampers and Pirelli Cinturato tyres were fitted. There were other possibilities, including fitting two twin-choke Weber carburettors, and some reports spoke also of 118bhp or 132bhp versions. Rudd's advertising showed his wire wheel conversions for the saloon and coupé models but stopped

VOLVO, 4-sitzige CABRIOLETS

Carosserie Jacques Coune 286 avenue de la Couronne Bruxelles

Jacques Coune in Brussels built a handful of his 120-based four-seater convertibles (above), but only one example was built of the Coune two-seater (right).

British modification: the engine bay of a Ruddspeed-tuned 120 series.

short of promoting a wire-wheeled estate! At least one original Ruddspeed-tuned car is still known to exist, but the number of cars converted is not recorded.

Volvo itself offered a variety of tuning kits for the B18 and B20 engines in the 1960s and 1970s, while in Germany the Frankfurt importers from 1962 offered a special 122SR model fitted with a tuned engine as well as specialised equipment – including a limited-slip differential, stiffer suspension, two driving lamps and extra instruments – aimed at owners who wanted to go saloon car racing or rallying. Power rose from an initial 90bhp to 128bhp for later versions, comparable to the output obtainable with the Volvo tuning kit for the B18 engine.

BIRTH OF THE P1800

Volvo's first attempt at entering the hitherto untested sports car market began its gestation period in 1953 when Assar Gabrielsson visited the USA with the intention of assessing the possibility of exporting Volvo cars to that country. His primary object reached fulfilment in 1955, when the first PV444s arrived in North America. However, during the 1953 visit he was also able to see for himself the impact of small European sports cars, especially in California. MG and Jaguar were household names, Austin-Healey and Triumph were just beginning to arrive, while more obscure makes available included Cisitalia, Siata and Simca-Gordini. Of the contemporary American cars, the then new Chevrolet Corvette made an impression with its novel glass-fibre body.

Gabrielsson visited the Californian Glasspar company, which had pioneered the use of glass-fibre for boats and latterly cars, including the improbably-named Willys-based Woodill Wildfire and the Kaiser-Darrin, both open two-seaters. Gabrielsson commissioned Glasspar to design, develop and produce a glass-fibre body to fit a

First thoughts of a Volvo sports car resulted in the glass-fibre P1900, here in its 1954 form with flat windscreen, fixed side windows and no hood. The P1900 had a full complement of instruments, including an oil temperature gauge – but that gear lever would have been more at home in a Volvo truck! Only 67 P1900s were made.

A rare colour shot from Volvo's archive of what is probably the first Italian-built P1800 prototype (above), painted grey, with its over-ornate wheel trims and golden

'V' on the radiator grille. Chassis 03 (below) of the production P1900s, now in the collection of Danish Volvo dealer and car collector Ole Sommer (seen here, left, in 1977).

chassis with a wheelbase of 2400mm (94.5in). The styling was the work of Glasspar founder Bill Tritt. Drawings were quickly completed and were despatched to Sweden, with instructions from Gabrielsson for Gothenburg to develop a new chassis for the car. This featured a combination of tubular and box-section members, while mechanical components were taken from the PV444 saloon. The 1.4-litre engine was fitted with two SU carburettors, becoming the B14B version that was also later fitted in PV444 'California' and Sport models. It developed 70bhp. The gearbox was the usual Volvo three-speed unit, with a specially cranked gear lever. The steering column was lowered almost to the horizontal.

The original Glasspar body had a panoramic dog's leg windscreen and an integral hard top, and American mock wire wheel hub caps were fitted. The most striking styling feature was the large oval radiator grille, reminiscent of a jet engine air intake. While Glasspar was contracted to supply 20 bodies, the intention was that Volvo would then take over body manufacture.

When this car, the P1900, was first shown to the public in June 1954, some styling changes had already been made. The windscreen was flat, with a slim frame. The car was now a roadster, supplied with a detachable hard top but no hood. The side windows were fixed and normal PV444 hub caps were fitted. The boot lid was of the clamshell type, sitting on top of the body line. As the car was to be fitted with the newest Swedish Trelleborg tubeless 'Safe-T' tyres, Volvo did not intend to supply a spare wheel, believing the tyres to be puncture proof. Billed as the Volvo Sport, the car was stated to be going into production in the autumn of 1954 at the rate of one per day, being reserved for export. It is not certain where the P1900 designation came from – the engine was of only 1414cc but it appears that the kerb weight of the car was around 1900lb!

No production followed in 1954 or even 1955, although prototypes were extensively tested in Sweden and abroad. One car at least was fitted with a ZF five-speed gearbox, and subsequently tried by *The Autocar*. The final production model was only available in early 1956 and then incorporated a number of further changes. The cockpit was lengthened to allow for occasional seats in the rear. A normal hood was fitted, a spare wheel was now supplied, and the windscreen was curved and fitted in a thicker frame. There were wind-down windows and swivelling quarterlights in the doors, and also rear quarterlights that hinged down rearwards. A conventional flush boot lid was fitted. No full road test of the car

One of the first pictures released of the P1800 in 1959. Still unnamed, it was described as 'an elegant sports car...designed by Volvo'.

appears to have been carried out in either Europe or North America but press reports suggested a top speed of around 96mph (155kph).

Only 44 cars were made in 1956, while in 1957 production amounted to a mere 23 units. Of the total production of 67, 27 are believed to have been sold in the USA, 38 in Sweden, with the remaining two cars going to Brazil and Belgium. The problem with the car was that it was evidently not going to pay its way. The bodies were built literally by hand, glass-fibre technology was in its infancy, and build quality was suspect.

Even if it had been possible to step up production – and 67 cars was the equivalent of a rather bad day's output from the MG factory – it seems doubtful that the car would have sold in any numbers. It is difficult to find an actual sales price for the car, but when Volvos were first shown in Britain at Earls Court in 1956, the display included a P1900 and an English-language leaflet was produced to mark the occasion. The tentative price of £2100, inflated by import duty and purchase tax, compared with the most expensive Jaguar XK140 at £1900 and an MGA Roadster at well below £1000…

In 1956, when Assar Gabrielsson finally went into well-earned retirement, Gunnar Engellau became Volvo's new boss at a time when the Amazon was just being

This interior from an early prototype survived on production models with few modifications. The dashboard may have been influenced by contemporary American designs. Buck Rogers would have felt quite at home...

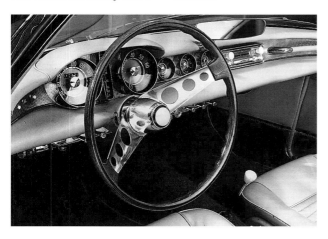

readied for production. Engellau took the opportunity to take a P1900 away for a weekend's test drive, and came back on the Monday morning to announce his decision that the car would have to go. In its short life the car had achieved little for Volvo. It was not even dramatic enough to be much of an image-builder, even if Volvo had wanted to become seen as a sports car maker. Its only lasting impact came later, as the rarest and most sought-after classic Volvo. In fact most of the cars still exist, cherished by Volvo fans in Sweden and the USA.

How much did the P1900 contribute to the genesis of the later P1800? Its sad and short-lived history must still have been fresh in the memory of Engellau and his colleagues when in 1957 they decided to have another go at building a sporting Volvo. If in 1953 the inspiration for the P1900 had come from British sports cars, the goalposts had effectively moved in 1955 when Volkswagen introduced the Karmann-Ghia, a pretty, Italian-designed but non-sporting coupé based on tried

Never mind the F-registration from the 1967-68 period: this is a very authentic example (above) of the 1961-63 P1800 as built by Jensen in Britain. The distinctive rear end shows effective use of bright trim strips to accentuate the lines. Contemporary shot (left) of one of the first batch of British-built P1800s, brought back to Gothenburg. Any car with these 'cowhorn' front bumpers is now much sought-after.

Under the front-hinged bonnet of an early P1800 lies this twin-SU 1780cc engine, first of the five-main bearing B18 series.

The front badge of the P1800 (below left) was this stylised shield with a rendering of the traditional symbol for iron. The Volvo script on the rear quarter pillars (below right) displayed stripes in Sweden's national blue and yellow colours.

and trusted family saloon mechanicals. Volvo decided to follow in the footsteps of Volkswagen and other European manufacturers by commissioning an Italian design, apparently somewhat to the irritation of Wilsgaard, its own chief designer. So Volvo approached Ghia, although it appears that much of the initial design work was undertaken by Frua.

Here the joker entered the pack. Helmer Petterson, who had been instrumental in the development of the PV444 and still acted as a consultant to Volvo, had a son, Pelle, who was just finishing his industrial design course. He would later find fame as a boat designer and yachtsman. Engellau had entrusted Petterson senior with the task of commissioning the early coupé sketches from Italian designers that in due course resulted in four proposals, two each from Ghia and Frua. But Petterson slipped a fifth design into the portfolio for Engellau to choose from, and, unknown to the Volvo boss, it was by Pelle Petterson. Only after Engellau had chosen the Petterson design was this particular cat let out of the bag. When Engellau had simmered down, the situation was resolved with Frua being asked to develop a prototype car based on Pelle's design, while the young designer himself was temporarily installed in Frua's studio.

The car that emerged in December 1957 was obviously styled in the contemporary Italian manner, yet was sufficiently unique and distinctive to lend credence to the story that the germ of the design had come from a young, unknown Swedish industrial designer. It was a classic coupé shape, with a long bonnet, short and low greenhouse, and short boot. As the car was to have a unitary body, based on a 120 series floorpan with a shortened wheelbase, Volvo did not contemplate making a drophead variant (although such conversions were later to be briefly marketed in both Britain and in the USA,

The wheel trims on the original production model were somewhat toned down from those on the prototypes, and now much sought-after. The rear seats were never intended for other than very occasional use but there was a useful cubby hole above them. And, of course, the P1800 came with standard-fit seat belts!

Compared with the prototype interior, production cars had differently-styled seats, the lower dashboard rail was modified and the door trims had a contrast colour section. Lined with rubber matting, the boot was not the greatest asset of the P1800, and the horizontal spare wheel took up quite a bit of space.

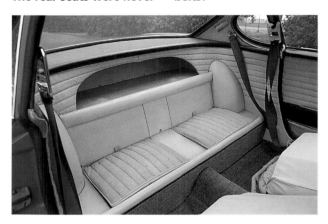

they tend to look much less distinctive than the Volvo original with its striking side window shape).

Up front, a bold oval egg-crate grille sat above two half bumpers of 'cowhorn' shape, a motif repeated also for the rear bumpers of the prototype. A distinctive chrome trim strip swept along each flank from headlamp up to the rear quarterlight. At the rear were chrome-trimmed tail fins, each presiding over a pair of small round lamp units, while the tail panel could be described as a counter stern, to borrow a term from the world of naval architecture that was Pelle's forte.

The interior was luxurious with a multi-colour trim scheme. There was a full set of instruments arranged along a shelf in front of the driver, a sports steering wheel with two drilled alloy spokes, and Volvo's first remote

control gearchange. There were rather cramped occasional rear seats. Suspension and steering components were largely similar to the 120 series, but servo-assisted front disc brakes by Girling were fitted when the car officially emerged in 1961. At the same time it was also revealed that the new car had a 1780cc engine, the first of the five-bearing B18 series. In twin-SU form for the P1800 it was known as the B18B and gave 100bhp. An oil cooler was standard equipment. While the gearbox was Volvo's by then usual fully-synchronised four-speeder, the P1800 was the first Volvo to be offered with optional Laycock de Normanville overdrive.

However, this is getting a little ahead of the story. The first prototype, finished in a sombre metallic grey, was ready for Volvo to view in Turin at the beginning of

1958, and Engellau quickly committed to putting the car into production. Three prototypes were completed by Frua, the other two painted white and red respectively. All three cars were shipped to Sweden where some design fine-tuning was done, including a change to the exhaust tailpipes, which originally protruded through the tail panel, and the introduction of a simpler rear bumper and simpler one-piece rear lamps. When the car was first revealed to the public in 1959, original features such as a large 'V' on the radiator grille and 'turbo' wheel trims were still in evidence, but both were removed before production began.

Now that Volvo had decided to go ahead with the car, the problem was where to make it. At the time, the old Volvo factory at Lundby was full to bursting point, the new 120 series fighting for space with the PV544 that was still going strong. Following the example of Volkswagen, whose Karmann-Ghia coupé was made by Karmann at Osnabrück, Volvo decided to find outside suppliers who could manufacture the bodyshell and assemble the car. Initial overtures to German companies, including Karmann, proved fruitless, so Volvo went to Britain, where the Pressed Steel Company agreed to make the bodies in its new factory at Linwood in Scotland. Originally set up to make railway rolling stock, this later became the source for the Hillman Imp bodies. While PSC declined the opportunity of also carrying out final assembly of the car, it introduced Volvo to Jensen at West Bromwich, near Birmingham.

Apart from making its own cars in limited numbers, Jensen already had some experience of working as a contractor, having supplied BMC with fully-finished Austin-Healey bodies since 1953. When first approached by Volvo in late 1958, the company was still controlled by its founders, the by then ailing brothers Alan and Richard Jensen, but in 1959 they sold a controlling interest to the Norcross Group. This holding company could offer extra financial resources, which enabled Jensen to branch out into additional contract work. During 1959 Jensen became very much involved in final work on the P1800 prototypes, making the car ready for quantity production, although the company's role was only publicly acknowledged when the production cars were released in mid-1961.

The first time the public learned of the new Volvo coupé, however, had been more than two years earlier, as pictures were released in May 1959. The car in the metal was seen at the Brussels motor show in January 1960 and appeared again at the New York motor show in April. Arguably, this was all somewhat premature as production only got under way in the winter and spring of 1961.

The production logistics were fairly formidable. Raw bodyshells had to be freighted from Scotland down to the Midlands. Jensen then took over, carrying out paint, trim and final assembly, with a team of Volvo inspectors on hand. While many components apart from the body were sourced in Britain – it was estimated that more than 50 per cent of the car was of UK origin – there was still an American Spicer rear axle, the steering gear and the ignition system came from Germany, and the engine, gearbox and other components had to be shipped in from Sweden. For good measure the tyres – Pirelli Cinturato radials – were Italian, although these were later made by Pirelli in Britain. While it was the intention that cars should be despatched directly from West Bromwich to world markets, the first batch of 250 cars was shipped back 'home' to Sweden for quality control and final preparation before the new model went on sale.

This is a slightly later car, a 1963 model. Probably one of the first Swedish-built cars, it has the unusual combination of the early-type rear quarter pillar script badges with the 120 series wheel trims.

1800 SERIES IN DETAIL

When the P1800 finally came on the market in 1961, it was generally warmly welcomed. If there was any particular criticism of the car, it was that it already looked perhaps a little old-fashioned. For all its much-touted Italian styling – most contemporary commentators toed Volvo's party line and ascribed the design to Frua – it was clearly a child of the 1950s, with its rounded, flowing lines and small glass area, in marked contrast to the later crisp-edge creations from the likes of Pininfarina. The shape, however, was conceded to be of 'timeless simplicity'.

In the important American market the price of the standard model was fixed at $3795 (East Coast port of entry, without the optional overdrive), although this was soon increased to $3995. Volvo ran a series of

The 1965 model year cars had a new design of wheel with stainless steel hub caps, of the same type as found on the 120 series cars. From the front, the new one-piece grille pressing is evident on the 1965 car, and so is the new slim-line straight bumper with a rubbing strip.

One modification to the interior, introduced on 1964 models, was that the rear seat was given a folding backrest which converted into a luggage platform, with straps to retain your luggage.

The dashboard was unchanged apart from a new grab handle on the passenger side, but revised leather-faced seats now featured adjustable lumbar support. Leather wearing surfaces on the front seats featured on all 1800s except the first 1000 or so, which were trimmed entirely in vinyl.

Typical Volvo chassis number plate (above). The five-figure type code is, on this car, followed by the letter H for 'Höger' – meaning right-hand drive – and the series letter E for 1965 model year. Below the chassis number are the codes for paint and trim colours. Castellated 1800S badge (above right) was used from the start of production in Sweden in 1963.

advertisements featuring European exotica, including the long-defunct BMW 507, all of which had price tags between $10,000 and $13,000. The slogan was 'What's it like to own a $10,000 car? – Find out for $3995', but the company was careful to avoid any comparison with the $6000 Jaguar E-type coupé.

Much the same situation prevailed in Britain, where the P1800, complete with overdrive, was listed at £1837, substantially more expensive than British sports cars such as the MGA 1600 Mark II (£968), Sunbeam Alpine (£1014), Triumph TR4 (£1095) or Austin-Healey 3000 (£1202), but at least with a good margin to the E-type coupé (£2261). Simple price comparisons such as these, however, overlook the almost unique virtue of the P1800: it was a 2+2 grand touring coupé offering more accommodation, convenience and luxury than British roadsters. The nearest any British manufacturer in 1961 came to offering a strictly comparable car was AC with the Aceca coupé, a very limited production machine that cost £1890 in its cheapest form.

Better comparisons are perhaps possible in the 'neutral' Swiss market, where a P1800 cost Sfr 18,500 as against the Sfr 21,900 asked for the soon to be discontinued Mercedes-Benz 190SL, although a 'cooking' Porsche 356 1600 coupé was Sfr 1000 less than the Volvo. An E-type coupé cost Sfr 27,500, and the most expensive of the lesser British sports cars was the Austin-Healey 3000 at around Sfr 15,000. Still, as a true GT car of medium size, the Volvo, even internationally, occupied an almost unique market niche.

With a top speed of around 105mph (169kph), a 0-60mph time of just over 13sec and an overall fuel consumption of 24-30mpg, performance of the P1800 was adequate for the time, and not much different from the similar-sized but lighter MGB introduced in 1962. Road-holding and handling won general praise although it was noted that the car would roll somewhat when cornering, due perhaps to the fact that the suspension was softer than on most sports cars – which in turn endowed the car with a particularly comfortable ride. There was just a little understeer in the dry, more so on a wet surface where the car could change into power-induced oversteer and was apt to spin its rear wheels.

While the build quality solicited warm testimonials from many reporters – in the USA *Car and Driver* described the P1800 as 'the best car the Jensen brothers ever made' – there was some dissent, notably from Bill Boddy in *Motor Sport* who resorted to italics to express his view that 'I cannot help feeling ashamed, however, of faults in British workmanship which it is improbable the meticulous engineers at Goteberg (sic) would have permitted.' This, of course, was the fly in the ointment.

The Saint – or Roger Moore – with his chosen mount, in this case actually a 1967 or later model with the double-barred grille.

The 'meticulous engineers' at Gothenburg did have strong reservations about the quality of the early British-built cars, and resorted to putting in extra quality control inspectors in the Jensen factory. When the problem was analysed, many of the faults seemed to arise from poor preparation of the bodyshells as received unprimed from Linwood, coupled with the transportation and the periods of storage before the body was finally transformed into a complete car. Nor was Jensen entirely free of blame, with the quality of their sealing, paintwork and general assembly coming in for criticism.

When, in early 1963, Volvo was able partly to commission the big new Torslanda assembly plant into which 120 series production was transferred, the decision was made to move P1800 assembly back home, to the old Lundby factory. While the original contract with Jensen had called for 10,000 cars to be assembled in Britain, production at West Bromwich was terminated in March 1963 after only 6000 cars had been built. The parting was 'sweetened' by Volvo paying Jensen compensation for the loss of business.

Pressed Steel, however, continued to supply the bodyshell, even after the Linwood factory was sold to Rootes and thus later to Chrysler. Only in 1968-69 were the press tools shipped to Sweden and installed in Volvo's body plant at Olofström. In round figures, something like 30,000 cars had British-made bodyshells.

The start of assembly in Sweden was accompanied by minor changes to the car. The original, unique wheel

A period publicity shot of the revised 1965 model (right). The number plate and the setting are Danish; Volvo's photographers regularly roamed Scandinavia in search of attractive backdrops. Isn't it amazing what good car photographers can achieve by using very small suitcases (below)? There is, however, also a golf bag in this 1800 boot! The 1967 models featured this new grille (below right) with double bars. Sweden changed from driving on the left to driving on the right in 1967: has this 1800 driver become confused and decided to stick to the middle of the road?

trims were replaced by standard 120 series type hub caps. The model was re-named 1800S and given a new tail badge. The Volvo script on the rear quarter pillars disappeared after about 200 cars had been built, and there were amber lenses for the direction indicators except on US-bound cars. The engine was given a hotter camshaft and compression was raised to 10:1, with power increasing from 100bhp to 108bhp, top speed now being close to 110mph (177kph).

By now one legend had already been created round the Volvo. When, back in 1930, author Leslie Charteris for the first time put his gentleman-hero Simon Templar, 'The Saint', behind the wheel of a car, the chosen vehicle was the mythical silver-grey 'Hirondel' about whose origins we were left to wonder except that it was indubitably British. When, 30-odd years later, Lew Grade of Associated Television decided to bring 'The Saint' to the small screen with Roger Moore in the title role, the

The revised 1800E model (right) was new for the 1970 model year. Externally, the hallmarks were cast alloy wheels and ventilation air outlets on the rear wings, the one on the left combined with a new fuel filler flap. The 1800E grille (below) on 1970 and '71 models was still the double-bar type, but was fashionably decked out in matt black paint.

The Volvo badge at the front was of this castellated type...

...similar to the rear badge, which now read '1800E'.

first choice for his car was apparently a Jaguar E-type, but they were frustrated by a certain lack of interest and co-operation from the Coventry firm.

Purely by chance, Moore came across the Volvo P1800 in 1962, and within a week a white Volvo, 71 DXC, had been delivered to the TV company. The following year a second P1800, 77 GYL, was taken on for filming, and this car currently resides in Peter Nelson's ownership at the 'Cars of the Stars' museum in

Keswick. These Volvos starred in about 100 TV episodes and, as a bonus, Moore privately drove similar cars for many years. Corgi Toys also cashed in on the publicity by bringing out a version of its P1800 model as 'The Saint's Volvo', in white with 'The Saint' matchstick-man logo on the bonnet and Roger Moore figure inside. Corgi's sales of 1.2 million of these models were about four times as many as of its basic P1800 toy car.

Between 1963-69, the 1800S jogged along without

Missing in the colour photos of the 1971 P1800E is the grille-mounted B20 badge, which can be seen in this contemporary picture together with the new composite steel/alloy wheels with stainless steel trim rings.

Under the bonnet was this fuel-injected version of the new B20 engine, with the first signs of nightmarish modern engine plumbing.

major modifications but there were regular cosmetic retouches, usually introduced in August at the start of each model year. Volvo designated each model year by a series letter. The original Jensen-built cars had been Series A, and the first batch of Swedish-built cars in 1963 was Series B. C was skipped, and D indicated the 1964 model year cars. These were fitted with improved front seats with adjustable backrests, and there was a folding backrest to the rear seats. The overdrive was now standard equipment on all cars. For the 1965 model year (Series E), new pierced wheels with smaller stainless steel hub caps (shared with Volvo saloons) were fitted, the background to the central 'V' motif on the hub cap being black rather than red. A simpler but less distinctive pressed aluminium grille was fitted, and the 'cowhorn' front bumpers were replaced with straight bumpers; both front and rear bumpers were given a rubbing strip. The new seats had 120-style lumbar support. The original

No great change to the P1800E rear compartment apart from the air extractors on the quarter pillars. Front seat headrests were now standard. Note the embossed Volvo emblem in the centre of the backrest.

The P1800E featured an all-new dashboard with much clearer white-on-black dials, now also with round temperature gauges. The three-spoke steering wheel had been introduced on the 1969 models.

colours of white, red and grey were supplemented by light blue.

Series F cars for 1966 had an improved cylinder head with separate exhaust ports which helped to increase power output to 115bhp. Then the series letter system skipped quite a few to arrive at Series M for 1967, bringing the 1800 (and other models) into line with the series letter for the four-door 120 model. On these cars, the side trim strip was new, of slimmer section and

continuing in a straight line along the side of the car to above the rear wheel arch. The tail fin trim strip was unchanged, but linked up with an extended design of door handle. The front grille was fitted with double bars, horizontally and vertically.

The 1969 models, designated as Series S, had a new three-spoke steering wheel (quite different from the 123GT wheel) and a collapsible steering column, while new US safety legislation was also making itself felt in the

Safety was the inspiration for the padding on the three-spoke steering wheel – more important was the collapsible column.

The fuel-injected B20 engine, which gave an impressive 130bhp, also featured an alternator and slipping clutch for the radiator fan.

In 1969 P1800 body production moved from Pressed Steel in Britain back home to the by then Volvo-owned body plant at Olofström.

The one that got away. The experimental 'Rocket' had particularly dramatic rear end styling – but would it have made it as a Volvo?

provision on US-bound cars of headrests and different switchgear, and – as was the case for the 120 series – the first simple exhaust emission control systems.

In common with the 120 and 140 series saloon models, a new engine, the bored-out B20 of 1986cc, was also fitted to 1969 (Series S) models, with compression lowered to 9.5:1 and output quoted as 118bhp. Exhaust emission control was standard for all markets. Zenith-Stromberg carburettors were generally fitted, but SUs were still used on some cars. The oil cooler was

discontinued. Dual-circuit brakes were standardised for all markets. Despite the new engine, the model designation stayed as 1800S and only a B20 badge on the radiator grille revealed the difference externally.

The model's most important update came with the 1970 models (Series T), for which the engine was fitted with Bosch electronic fuel injection, the Jetronic system also used by Porsche. Together with a new camshaft, larger valves and a compression ratio of 10.5:1, this boosted output to 130bhp. How much this meant for the

The eventual production version of the P1800ES was more subdued and Volvo-like, yet the deep all-glass hatch was a striking and unique feature.

From the front there was little change for the P1800ES, but the vertical-bar radiator grille and the wheels were new.

The P1800ES interior had an even more luxurious feel with these opulent leather seats (below left), with built-in 'tombstone' headrests. The rear seats (below) were all new, with a style mirroring the front seats. The rear seat back folded to give increased luggage space.

performance of the car is questionable: *Motor* in Britain measured an average top speed of only 108mph (174kph) whereas other international publications spoke of over 120mph (190kph or more). A new ZF gearbox, shared with the 164 saloon, still had four speeds apart from the overdrive. Another mechanical improvement was that disc brakes were fitted all round, hiding behind new standard-fit composite wheels in alloy and steel.

Apart from the wheels, the new car, called the 1800E, could be distinguished by its matt black grille, while the presence of a new cabin through-flow ventilation system was indicated by small air vents on the rear wings, on the left-hand side combined with a repositioned fuel filler flap. Inside the car the dashboard style was all new, with redesigned white-on-black instruments set in a strip of imitation wood veneer in a matt black surround. The original rather 'jukeboxy' vertical oil and water temperature gauges of the capillary type were replaced by round dials. The thoroughly revised car was listed in Britain at £2254, which was felt to be expensive compared with a Jaguar E-type (£2351) or Reliant Scimitar GTE (£2019). In the crucial US market the price of an 1800E increased to about $4595.

On the 1971 models (Series U) Volvo reverted to its own four-speed gearbox, now suitably beefed-up to handle the power of the injection engine, instead of the ZF 'box. For the first time the 1800E was offered with the option of an automatic gearbox, the same Borg-Warner type 35 that was in use on Volvo's saloons.

For 1972 the model became Series W, with a new grille of matt black plastic with vertical bars. Wheels reverted to the pressed steel type as standard, with bright trim rings and bright dome finishers for the exposed wheel nuts. Tinted glass was fitted, while new seats were another luxury touch. Engine power was improved to 135bhp (SAE), although the emission control engine for North America had 10bhp less. However, production of the 1800E coupé came to an end on 22 June 1972, after a total of 39,406 cars of all types from 1961 to 1972 had been made. But one model of the 1800 series was still in production – the 1800ES that had been introduced a year earlier.

The 1800ES was the result of Volvo's search for a car to replace the 1800. This had been pursued with varying degrees of determination since the early 1960s, with Volvo stylist Wilsgaard and his colleagues proposing a variety of schemes. The fact that Volvo did not consider making a convertible 1800 prompted two outsiders to offer their own. In Britain, Radford built two such cars (one of which survives today) for the Volvo dealer in

Cast alloy wheels were replaced for 1800ES with new steel design, now with exposed wheel nuts, small centre cap and bright 'rimbellisher'.

Hull in 1965, but they were said to suffer from structural defects. In the USA, Volvoville of Long Island at around the same time converted an estimated 30-50 coupés to convertibles, for which they claimed an additional 6in of rear seat headroom with the top up – with the top down it would have been rather more! However, 1800 convertibles existing today are mainly latter-day conversions by private enthusiasts, as is the case for present-day 120 series convertibles.

An early alternative that Volvo did consider was a fastback version styled by Fissore in Italy, although the finished car was brought to Sweden for assessment and led to the construction at Gothenburg of a number of other proposals, some of fastback style, others of conventional coupé design. Their common feature was that all of them had radically different greenhouses but little modified bodies below the waistline – Volvo had taken to heart the criticism of the production model for looking old-fashioned with its small and low glass area. Sketches were then developed of 1800 derivatives that kept the windscreen and roof line of the standard car but had extended roofs in estate car style and almost vertical rear glass hatches. There was the 'Beachcar', the 'Hunting Car' and finally the 'Rocket', this last proposal featuring a rear end that was near oval in section, with a neatly-integrated rear bumper.

The scheme eventually adopted was not so extreme and managed to carry over the rear wings from the coupé. It did, however, feature the lengthened estate car

The big advantage of the 1800ES was this roomy luggage space, fully carpeted and with the spare wheel hidden under the floor.

type roof and the large unframed glass rear hatch. The car was signed off by Volvo in 1968 and prototype construction was undertaken by the Italian house of Coggiola. The model was introduced to the public in August 1971 as the 1800ES and, apart from the new body style, shared the features of the contemporary 1800E coupé, including the pressed-steel wheels and the new leather upholstered seats with integral headrests.

In Britain the car was inevitably and immediately compared with the Reliant Scimitar GTE, which had been on the market since October 1968 — although Volvo liked to argue that it had the idea before Ogle designed the Reliant! In Britain the 1800ES cost over £2600, while in the USA the price was more than $5000. Road tests mostly spoke of a top speed around the 112mph mark (180kph) — not a great improvement over the original 1961 car.

In general the 1800ES was felt to be a worthwhile improvement over the original. *Road & Track* described it as 'a successful conversion from dated GT to genuine sportswagon...a good, solid car but a crude and old-fashioned one'. *Motor* was critical of the driving position, the visibility, the very limited room in the rear seats and above all the interior noise level, and the magazine called the shape 'highly distinctive if hardly beautiful'. No matter, Volvo was again in the fortunate position of having an almost unique car in the marketplace, especially in the USA where the Reliant Scimitar was unknown. The 1800ES held a lot of appeal with its

combination of sporting performance and handling, and its 35 cu ft (1 cu m) load capacity was far superior to that of, for instance, the MGB GT. The 'sporting estate' concept was later adopted by Lancia for the Beta HPE of 1975, by which time the second-generation Ford Capri had also appeared complete with rear hatch. BMW pursued a similar ideal with the Touring version of the '02' series that had already been launched in 1971.

It was sad, therefore, that Volvo decided to discontinue the 1800ES after only two years in production. While the 1800E coupé had disappeared in June 1972, the 1973 models of the 1800ES (Series Y) cars had further small modifications, mostly on North American specification cars, which were fitted with impact-absorbing bumpers and had their engines, able to run on lead-free fuel, detuned to 112bhp. With further US safety and emissions standards in the offing, Volvo decided that with the limited sales of the model (5000 in the last model year, predominantly in the USA) there was little point in making further investments to modify the 1800ES to keep it abreast of new legislation, so on 27 June 1973 the last 1800ES came off the production line.

Some consideration was given to a successor. Coggiola, who had been involved in 1800ES development, displayed a very handsome coupé based on the 1800 at the 1971 Paris motor show, known as the Volvo ESC or the Volvo Viking. Zagato also tried its hand with a not dissimilar, if less pretty, coupé based on the 164 six-cylinder saloon. Back in Gothenburg, Wilsgaard had already designed and finished — and abandoned — the P172 which dated back to 1966-67. Not exactly a straightforward 1800 replacement, this was an elegant 2+2 based on the forthcoming 164 and would have taken Volvo into a new market sector, at that time dominated by the Mercedes-Benz coupés. This idea was quickly shelved, however, by an apprehensive Volvo management. Then there was the 262C of 1977-81, an idiosyncratic chopped-roof conversion built for Volvo by Bertone in Italy, followed by the much better-looking 780 of 1985, another exclusive two-door built by Bertone that lasted until 1990.

Also in 1985, Volvo did finally produce a car which could be seen as a replacement for the 1800ES. This car merits a niche in Volvo history of its own as the first front-wheel drive car to bear the name. It was a product of the Dutch Volvo company, the result of Volvo buying out the car interests of DAF ten years before. Like the 1800ES of old, the 480 had unique styling with an estate-like tail, developed in-house at Volvo's Dutch styling studio. The 1721cc engine was a joint Volvo-Renault

The profile of the P1800ES was still elegant – and it was not immediately obvious that this car was derived from a very different original. The dashboard and controls were carried over from the 1800E with no change.

Facing page. Volvo cutaway rendering shows all the salient features of the 1800ES, with the accent naturally on the rear of the car. A detail of the 1800ES grille, also used on the final year's production of the 1800E. Distinctive – but was it really an improvement over the original? The new model had new rear end badging, with a small one-piece Volvo name and this 1800ES badge.

project, and developed 120bhp in its most powerful turbocharged form.

The 480 lasted ten years in production, and while it was never marketed in the USA it achieved a respectable production figure of 77,000 cars, of which it is said that 22,000 were sold in Britain. Quirky styling and poor reliability ensured that it always had a mixed reputation. Richard Bremner obituarised it in *Car* magazine, describing its looks as 'like the result of a drug-hazed afternoon in an Amsterdam coffee shop' but finished up with a sneaking suspicion that here was 'a Volvo worth preserving. And there aren't many of them.' Enthusiasts for the classic Volvos – from the first PV444 to the last 1800ES – would undoubtedly disagree with the last sentiment…

The 480 was always a bit of a misfit, both in the Volvo range and in the wider car market, but it did pave the way for better things to come, such as the turbocharged front-wheel drive 850 of the 1990s, the car that brought Volvo back to its roots as a maker of 'family sports cars'. Promised for 1997 was the 850-based coupé and convertible range provisionally called the C7, styled by British-born RCA graduate Peter Horbury, who took over as Volvo's design director in 1991. Assisting on the engineering side was Tom Walkinshaw, Volvo's British partner in touring car racing. If the C7 were to be produced in Walkinshaw's factory near Banbury in Britain, the wheel of history really would come full circle, 35 years after the first P1800 was built in Britain…

VOLVO IN MOTOR SPORT

D espite the appearance of an original Volvo PV4 fabric saloon of the 1920s in the film *Monte Carlo or Bust*, the sporting career of the make was strictly a post-war phenomenon, and the actual works rally team operated for only about a decade. Volvo's finest years in the sport were from 1958 to 1966, a period which, incidentally, also saw the greatest successes for BMC's works rally team. Like BMC, Volvo was amply rewarded, winning the European Rally Championship three times, in 1958, 1963 and 1964. Of the individual victories, those scored in the RAC Rally in 1963 and 1964, and the Safari in 1965, made perhaps the greatest impact on the international scene.

Where it (almost) all began: Gunnar Andersson takes a yump in the PV444 on his way to victory in the 1958 Midnight Sun Rally.

Scandinavia tends to breed expert rally drivers, the combination of severe winters and plenty of loose-surfaced forest roads obviously bringing out the best in these guys. Since the World Drivers' Championship was instituted by the FIA in 1978, the majority of titles have been taken by Swedish or Finnish drivers. In the 1960s, the abilities of Timo Makinen and Rauno Aaltonen earned them not only the 'Flying Finns' nickname but brought memorable victories for the BMC Mini

An interesting shot of the Parc Fermé at Monaco after the 1959 Monte Carlo Rally, with a pair of 120 series cars to the fore, and at least one PV down in the background. Number 233 was the mount of Andersson and Karlsson, who came 28th overall.

Putting the message across to the Argentinians – Gunnar Andersson piloting the winning PV544 in the 1960 Gran Premio Internacional road race.

Coopers. Saab, of course, had a 'Flying Swede' in the shape of Erik Carlsson, while Volvo was well served, too, by the native breed of driver – notably Gunnar Andersson, Ewy Rosqvist, Carl-Magnus Skogh, Tom Trana and Silvia Österberg. And Hannu Mikkola, World Cup Rally winner and 1983 World Champion, began his competition career in Volvos.

The Volvo became such a successful rally car primarily because of its ruggedness and strength, rather than any particularly high performance, although later PV544s were at times indecently quick for all their 'grannie' looks. It is typical that most Volvo victories were earned in loose-surface rallies, in Scandinavia and in the RAC, apart from the Safari Rally. Volvos tended to do less well in the faster tarmac-based events but even here could pull off the occasional surprise. Of the individual models, the old PV warhorse always performed best, being the lighter and more 'chuckable' car, but the 120 series also had its moments even if its active career was cut short when Volvo pulled out of rallying in 1966. Both benefited from the B18 engine's responsiveness to tuning (where regulations allowed), although some *cognoscenti* preferred, and continue to prefer, the B16 engine, which is more willing to rev with its three-bearing crankshaft. The 1800 coupé was also briefly tried in rallying in 1961 but these entries did not go beyond the purely experimental stage.

Because Volvo originally had little interest in motor sport, it was at first left to private drivers to fly the flag. An early appearance of a PV444 in international rallying came in the first post-war Monte Carlo in January 1949 when the intrepid trio of Messrs Ohlsson, Carstedt and Cederholm successfully finished the rally, and when they repeated the entry in the following year they actually came 12th overall – not a bad performance for a modest-engined family saloon. Although there were usually a few Volvos in this premier European rally every year in the early 1950s, it was not until 1958 that the make would achieve a better placing. Of other early results, Margerita Melin deserves a mention for winning the Ladies' Cup in the 1952 Swedish Rally, more poetically known as 'The Rally to the Midnight Sun'. In her PV444 she beat all other women entrants, including the more famous Greta Molander in a Saab 92.

In the 1953 Midnight Sun Rally, Backland and Broberg were class winners, a performance they repeated in the Norwegian Viking Rally in 1954. The PV444 came to the notice of a wider European audience when the enthusiastic Belgian importer decided in 1956 to enter a team of four cars in the Liège-Rome-Liège Rally, the famed Marathon de la Route. This resulted in a remarkable eighth place overall for Harris and Jacquemin, and Volvo duly collected the team prize with other finishers in 21st, 22nd and 23rd places. The focus shifted back to Scandinavia in 1957, where the Jansson brothers won the Midnight Sun Rally, while PV444s were first and second in the Viking Rally, Grøndal/Berntsen followed home by Ingier/Fløysvik.

Perhaps not unconnected with the fact that old man Assar Gabrielsson retired in 1956 and was replaced by

By 1961, Swedish cars were well-established contenders in the RAC Rally. While Erik Carlsson won for Saab, the PV544 of Andersson and British co-driver Johns finished a creditable sixth overall. By contrast poor Ewy Rosqvist struggled to finish the event, in one of the rare rally appearances of the P1800.

Gunnar Engellau, Volvo's view of competitions began to change. The company's best period in rallying started in 1958, when Gunnar Andersson came to the fore and the works team was officially established. Even before these events, at the start of the year Volvos suddenly burst forth on the European rally scene in the Monte Carlo Rally. Five PV444s were entered, crewed mostly by a medley of Scandinavian privateers, but it was the German entry of Löffler and Johansson who in the words of *The Autocar* were 'tipped as likely winners' of 'one of the toughest of all Monte Carlo Rallies'. Of 303 starters, only 59 figured in the final result list, after battles with snow and ice throughout France. Löffler and Johansson finished fourth overall, won the 'category 1' 2-litre class, and together with the other two finishing Volvos collected the Charles Faroux trophy as the team award. Not surprisingly, in the following years an awful lot of Volvos were entered in each Monte Carlo Rally…

By 1963 the works team was increasingly using the two-door 122S/B18. Here is the woman pair of Silvia Österberg and Inga Edenring on the Monte.

Gunnar Andersson was a 30-year-old car mechanic who ran his own workshop in Gothenburg. He was apparently not entirely without means as he had begun his competition career in a Jaguar XK120 in 1953, while later he used a Fiat 1100 before buying his first Volvo in 1957. He had this fitted with the US twin-carburettor engine, and planned an ambitious programme for 1958. His first event – and the first time he had rallied outside Scandinavia – was in the Acropolis Rally, where he finished third. In the Dutch Tulip Rally he led the field for a time but dropped back, as another PV444, driven by German privateers Kolwes and Lautmann, went on to win the rally. After Andersson had gained another third place in the German Rally, he was approached by Gunnar Engellau with the suggestion that he might like to come and work for Volvo. Before the starting date of his contract, Andersson had won the Midnight Sun Rally outright. Presumably no other references were required…

Then there were two set-backs as Andersson retired from both the Alpine Rally and from the Liège-Rome-Liège – in both cases the brakes wore out and caused him to crash. These disappointments were more than made up for when in July Andersson won the Adriatic Rally in Yugoslavia outright, while at the end of the season he finished second in the Viking Rally, where the winner

was Norwegian Hans Ingier – also in a PV444. With two wins, a second place and two third places, Andersson became the European Rally Champion of 1958. In addition, there were two other major wins for Volvo, so the make would comfortably have won a manufacturers' championship (which was only instituted in 1968).

The 1959 season was rather less spectacular, but 13 of the 23 Volvos entered in the Monte Carlo Rally finished, with Bengtson and Lohmander in sixth place. The '59 Monte was also the first major international event for the 120 series, with examples of this model finishing 28th and 44th overall. In his dual capacity as Volvo works driver and team manager, Andersson now had a promising colleague in Ewy Rosqvist, who won the Ladies' Cup in the Midnight Sun, Adriatic and Viking rallies, making her the European Ladies' Rally Champion of the year, her mount throughout the season one of the new PV544 models. A similar car was used by Hans Ingier, who won his second consecutive Viking Rally and came second to Callbo in another Volvo in the Finnish 1000 Lakes Rally.

Ewy Rosqvist could not repeat her championship in 1960, when she had to give best to Pat Moss in the Austin-Healey 3000, but Gunnar Andersson found his form again by winning the German Rally outright, finishing third in the Midnight Sun and Viking rallies,

Despite some evident damage to the PV544, skill and determination brought victory for Tom Trana (above) in the 1963 RAC Rally. Also snapped on the 1963 RAC Rally is Volvo's team leader Gunnar Andersson (right) in another of the works PV544s.

There was still some life left in the PV544 in 1964 (above left). Here Carl-Magnus Skogh lets the tail hang out on his way to ninth place in the Monte Carlo Rally. Skogh again (above), in the 1965 Acropolis Rally. He was the eventual winner, a high point in the European rally career of the 120 series. Hannu Mikkola (left), possibly the greatest rally driver ever, began his illustrious career with a PV544 in 1965.

and fourth in the 1000 Lakes. However, he scored a far more spectacular victory in the Gran Premio event in Argentina. Whether this was a rally or a fast road race is open to discussion, but Andersson averaged nearly 72mph (116kph) for almost 40 hours' driving, more than one hour ahead of the next car, on this 4623km (2873 miles) event. It was the first time that a European car had won this event, described as the toughest in the world. Incidentally, 1960 saw another appearance of a 120 series in a major rally, as the French crew of Morel and

Lemerle took a 122S from Warsaw through to a 56th place in the Monte Carlo Rally. Of 26 Volvos entered that year, none could manage better than 27th overall.

While the PV544 was still the regular Volvo rally car, in 1961 it was decided to have a go with the new P1800 coupé. There was also a new driver, Tom Trana, in the Volvo team. He held on to second place with his P1800 in the Midnight Sun Rally but had to retire when the clutch gave out. Ewy Rosqvist's turn in the P1800 came in the RAC Rally: she holed the fuel tank on a special

Tom Trana (above) getting along nicely on the 1965 Acropolis Rally. The Singh brothers, Joginder and Jaswant, scored one of the most memorable Volvo victories in the 1965 East African Safari rally (right, above and below).

stage in Scotland but was able to bring the car to the finish, scoring valuable points in the ladies' championship, which in fact she won handsomely in 1961, taking ladies' cups in seven out of 11 rallies entered. Gunnar Andersson himself drove a P1800 in the Liège-Rome-Liège but collided with a non-competing car, another Volvo team driver also ending in the resulting pile-up.

There were, in fact, no outright wins at all for Volvo in 1961. A Monte Carlo entry of 24 Volvos had as its best result a 14th place for Andersson and co-driver Lohmander. Andersson's best results with the PV544 were second in the Acropolis and third in the German Rally, while he was fourth in Poland, fifth in Finland and sixth in the RAC. However, when the points scores were added up at the end of the season, he was still placed second in the European Drivers' Championship.

Ewy Rosqvist decided to leave the Volvo team in 1962, going off in search of pastures new at Mercedes-Benz, her place as Volvo's leading lady being taken by Silvia Österberg. This was the year when the 120 series made its proper debut with the works rally team.

In the 1966 RAC Rally, Tom Trana – by now having the status of a private entry – could not manage to score a third victory, but nevertheless took his 122S to a fine third place.

After starting in Finnish rallying with a PV544, Hannu Mikkola changed to this 120 series car for 1966. A Volvo in its proper habitat – raising dust in the Scandinavian forests.

However, before this Andersson and Karlsson had finished in sixth place in the Monte Carlo Rally, Andersson's personal best ever in this event. His first outing in the 122S came in the Tulip Rally, where he was rewarded with a fine second place. He followed this up with a class win in the RAC Rally where new girl Österberg followed him home, also in a 122S. In the Marathon de la Route, Belgian driver Patte finished third with his 122S. Using the PV544, Andersson was sixth in the Acropolis, while on the other side of the world Volvos took second places in the Argentine Gran Premio and the Canadian Shell 4000 Rally.

The team hedged its bets again in 1963 and continued to use the PV544s as well as the 122S cars. Volvos finished in eighth and ninth places in the Monte Carlo Rally. Best personal results for Gunnar Andersson were second in the Acropolis and Polish rallies, and a third in the Tulip, all of them in the 122S. In fact, of eight major class wins in European rallies in 1963, five were with the new model. Although again without any outright wins, Andersson accumulated enough points to take the European Championship for a second time, while Silvia Österberg was the European ladies' champion and also won the Scandinavian rally championship (without gender qualification). In various non-championship rallies, there were Volvo wins in five smaller events in Sweden and Germany, and as far afield as the South African International Rally.

Everything else, however, was overshadowed when Tom Trana won the 1963 RAC Rally in his PV544. By now the British were quite resigned to seeing the Swedes dominate their national rally, but after three victories in a row for Erik Carlsson and his Saab, it must at least have been a change to see the other Swedish car at the fore. This was the start of Volvo's finest period in rallying…

The next year, 1964, was to be Trana's *annus mirabilis*. While it would have seemed more relevant for Volvo to have concentrated on using the 120 series in rallies, as this was now the most important production model, Trana doggedly stuck to the old faithful PV544, now almost at the end of the production run. How effective a tool this was in the right hands was proved by Trana repeating his win in the RAC, and also coming first in the Acropolis and Midnight Sun rallies, apart from a second place in the 1000 Lakes and a sixth in the Monte Carlo – where he put up excellent times on most of the special stages. Now it was Trana's turn to take the crown as the European Rally Champion.

This was also the year when Volvo completely dominated the Canadian Shell 4000 Rally with the 122S model. Ten Volvos started in 1964, ten finished, and they won all four major categories in the rally. Klaus Ross and John Bird were outright winners, while Olivier Gendebien, famous for his four Le Mans victories, came fourth. Naturally, the Volvos also took the team award. On the other hand, a major effort in the East African

Now in a 120 series car, Joginder Singh finished third in the 1966 Safari. A 'lion' came first, in the form of a Peugeot...

Joginder Singh's loyalty to Volvo yielded fourth place on the 1967 Safari – but two more victories in the 1970s made him one of the great Safari legends.

Safari Rally misfired badly: all the Volvos retired, with Trana crashing at an early stage. Trana's car was sold locally to one Joginder Singh, of whom we shall hear more.

The 1965 season started well with Carl-Magnus Skogh winning the Acropolis Rally for the works team in his 122S – but this was to be the only major European rally victory for the model. Trana and co-driver Thermaenius won the Midnight Sun Rally in a PV544. Then, sadly, the team was struck by tragedy. Two 122S cars were entered in the Gulf London Rally, but Trana collided with a non-competitor and Thermaenius was killed. Team-mates Skogh and Berggren withdrew as a mark of respect. Although Trana was later cleared of any blame by a British court, the Volvo entries were withdrawn altogether from the RAC Rally.

A few thousand miles to the south, Joginder Singh had managed to straighten out Trana's battered PV544 from the previous year's Safari Rally, and entered it in the 1965 rally with his brother Jaswant as co-driver. They won outright, and also came home first in the Ugandan

and Tanganyikan rallies, becoming effectively East African rally champions for the year. Joginder Singh was then invited to join the Volvo works team in Europe.

Singh, Andersson, Skogh and Trana were on the Acropolis Rally in May 1966, all in 122S cars, when tragedy struck again. A Volvo service car collided with a Greek lorry whose driver had fallen asleep, and three Volvo mechanics were killed. The team withdrew from the rally, and later in the year Volvo announced that it was temporarily withdrawing the works team from rallying. Before this, Trana and Andreasson had come third in their 122S in the Midnight Sun Rally, on which Singh had another drive for the works team. Trana also came second in the 1000 Lakes and – as a private entrant – third in the RAC Rally. Joginder Singh returned to Kenya where he and Bhardwaj finished third with a 122S in the Safari Rally. Meanwhile, a young Finnish driver

Common sight in British saloon car racing around 1960 (above left): a B16-engined 122S saloon with a Riley in hot pursuit. Les Leston was one British driver who changed from Riley to Volvo. Trana in a 122S at Brands Hatch (above right) in a damp-looking six-hour saloon car race in 1963 – with co-driver Skogh the result was a class win. This wonderfully varied grid (left) is the start of the 1964 Sebring 12-hours.

called Hannu Mikkola had come out in local rallying, cutting his teeth on a 122S. He was second in the Finnish rally championship and, in 1967, would come third overall in the 1000 Lakes. He continued to drive awhile for the Finnish Volvo importer before eventually joining the Ford team and moving on to bigger international events and a brilliant career.

While the PV544 went out in a blaze of glory, the RAC and Safari wins coming when the model was at the end of its career, the 120 series never really had a chance to become fully developed as a rally car. In any case, as BMC was also soon to find out, the world of rallying was about to change: the dominant rally car of 1968 was the Porsche 911, rally cars became more and more specialised, and eventually rallying would be opened up to limited-production Group 4 Grand Touring racing cars. Things quickly reached the point where an ordinary family saloon car no longer had any realistic chance of winning a major rally.

Volvo's record in track racing was far more patchy

and it was unusual for the parent company to support such activities, but more often than not private teams and drivers put up a good show, sometimes aided and abetted by local Volvo importers and dealers. In Sweden, the rest of Scandinavia, Germany, Britain and the USA, it was far from uncommon to see Volvos in saloon car racing, even filling the complete grid in their home territory.

Some importers found that race appearances were an excellent way of insuring publicity when they started to bring in Volvos. When Volvo first established a foothold on the US west coast, one Ron Pearson entered his PV444 in production car racing in California in 1956 and promptly took four firsts in the 1500cc class. Volvos appeared in the 'Little Le Mans' 10-hour endurance race at Lime Rock in Connecticut, taking the first five places in 1957 and a 1-2-3 in 1958. Art Riley was the winning driver on both occasions. He made it a hat-trick with a third victory in 1961, and also ran the car in a number of SCCA races – he won one event over a field of 18 MGAs! Later on, the 120 series was raced in the USA,

In the 1963 Taunus hillclimb (above), Seufert seems determined to 'wipe' out the opposition. At the Nürburgring in 1964 (above right), most of the Volvos seem to be at the back of the grid. Very much at the end of the active career of the 120 series in European rallying, the faithful German Volvo driver Kolwes still had a go in the 1967 Monte Carlo Rally (right).

including at least one appearance in the Daytona 24-hour race, while the 1800 coupé was seen at Daytona as well as at Sebring. In 1966, an 1800 was the SCCA Group F production car champion.

In 1958 Volvo brought none other than Jo Bonnier to England, where he drove a PV444 to a class win in the *Daily Express* touring car race at Silverstone. In 1959, Gunnar Andersson and Bengtsson came over to race the new 122S in the BRDC event at Silverstone, and came first and second in class. Their example inspired several British drivers to take up Volvos; Les Leston got a PV544 to replace his Riley, and 120 series cars became a regular sight in British touring car racing.

Back home in Sweden, before Tom Trana was signed on as a works driver he and Gunnar Andersson used to battle it out in local saloon car races. Trana was then brought on board and, for 1963, given the task of getting a class win in the European Touring Car Championship. He duly achieved the 2-litre class win, along the way taking a class win with Skogh in the 6-hour saloon car

race at Brands Hatch, and also made his mark in German racing. Already in 1961 in Germany, local driver Josef Maassen had become the national touring car champion with a 122S, while another leading exponent was Jochen Neerpasch, who sometimes co-drove with Skogh from the works team. In 1963, there were Volvo class wins in both the 6-hour and 12-hour races at the Nürburgring, and a third overall place in the longer race. As at this time Volvos were raced with both the B16 engine in the 1600cc class and the B18 engines in the 2000cc class, they had a total of four class wins in these two races.

On the Scandinavian home front, Volvos were dominant in ice racing which for obvious reasons is a sport not much practised elsewhere in Europe. Another less common and now all but forgotten form of motor sport was economy runs, often sponsored by Mobil. While there was usually no overall winner of these events, Volvos tended to do well in their class, and in 1963 alone had class wins in economy runs in Denmark, Norway and France.

VOLVOS TODAY

Like old soldiers, old Volvos never seem to die – they just keep rolling along. A recent estimate suggests that half of the Amazons sold in the Swedish home market are still on the road, and Volvos of all sorts are among the most frequently encountered classic cars throughout Scandinavia, offering ample testimony in support of Volvo's claims for long life and reliability. The most unlikely scene in the film *Four Weddings and a Funeral* may be the opening sequence where Hugh Grant's 122S refuses to start…

These Volvos have a strong and devoted following in the classic car world, not only in Scandinavia but in many European countries, particularly Britain, Germany, the Netherlands and Belgium. They are also extremely popular in North America, where their most famous adherent is General Colin Powell. In his autobiography, the General tells how as a young officer he was in the habit of supplementing his pay by repairing Volvos and selling them on, with about 30 cars passing through his hands. He was, however, refused a trader's licence as Fort Myers was considered an inappropriate address. Somehow, the famous rhetorical question once asked about President Nixon – 'Would you buy a used car from this man?' – springs to mind. Powell's pride and joy today is apparently a restored 122S saloon, so he was less than impressed when, at his official retirement as Chief of Joint Staffs, President Clinton presented him with an unrestored Volvo. Presumably this was the moment when the General decided to give his support to the Republican party…

For anyone contemplating buying a used 120 series, regardless of who it is from, there is actually comparatively little to worry about. The mechanical parts are fairly bullet-proof, with engines capable of very high mileages – 150,000 miles is considered common – before overhauls become necessary. However, sooner or later worn valve guides, worn bores or broken piston rings betray their presence by blue smoke, which is an indicator that some action is necessary. The original camshaft timing gear was made with fibre teeth which eventually break away from the steel hub, making a knocking sound, but Volvo replacement all-steel gears are available. The camshaft lobes will wear. Other points to watch are whether the correct three-row radiator is fitted rather than an inadequate two-row replacement, and whether the original Volvo oil filter is fitted as this has a special valve which allows free circulation from start-up.

Engine rebuilds are not too expensive as many parts can often be re-used. The B18 and B20 engines share many parts which are still freely available, but parts availability is not quite so good for the earlier B16 engine. Some 120 series cars have been fitted with B20 engines from 140 series cars, or even the later B21/B23 engines. Cars have also been fitted with complete fuel injection systems from 140 models. In the 1960s, Volvo offered a 128bhp tuning kit for the B18 engine and later a range of kits for the B20 engine, with 140bhp being available if two twin-choke Solex carburettors were fitted. For racing, the basic B20 engine could be (and frequently was) persuaded to give up to 180bhp, if not more. Some enthusiasts still carry out tuning work on these cars. In Scandinavia they have even been converted to other engines including the straight-six 3-litre from the Volvo 164 or the ubiquitous Rover 3.5-litre V8, in defiance of Swedish Ministry of Transport car examiners!

Gearboxes are quite as long-lived as engines. While very many cars sold in Britain were fitted with the overdrive, any car that is not so equipped can be converted, and the overdrive units are generally also reliable. The rear axles last equally well but will probably become rather noisy on estate cars sooner than saloons. Half shafts are reckoned to be a weak point, especially on cars with tuned engines, or on high-mileage cars if the potential of the still-willing engine is used to the full.

The double wishbone front suspension is simple and sturdy, like the rest of the chassis parts. Bushes, especially the rubber bushes on the upper wishbones, should be checked, as well as the top and bottom ball joints. Wear is more likely to occur if wider-than-standard wheels and tyres are fitted, as is often done to improve handling. Pre-1965 cars have grease points on the track rod and track rod ends, the upper ball joint and the steering arm. On

This early saloon – by the two-tone colour scheme a pre-1961 B16 engined car – seems to have withstood the ravages of time remarkably well.

Inner front wings and their box sections are a troublesome 1800 rust area, and replacement panels have yet to become available.

the rear suspension, the rust-prone trailing arms on cars up to mid-1966 should be checked. Stiffer rear springs and shock absorbers are available and are recommended for better handling. On estate cars, worn bushes in the rear radius arms may cause the arms to crack.

Neither steering nor brakes are likely to give much trouble. On cars with front discs (from 1964) the brakes are substantially over-dimensioned, and, if anything, they are likely to seize up from under use, especially on cars that are left to stand for extended periods. Found on some models for 1964, the servo became standard on all cars in 1966, while the late 120 series cars with the B20 engine also have dual-circuit brakes. A point to note is that a special puller is required to remove the rear brake drums and hubs.

Much of what has been said about the mechanicals of the 120 series also applies to the 1800s, but there are special points to watch out for, such as the Girling servo fitted to early Jensen-built cars no longer being available. The fuel injection system on cars built between 1969-73 is generally reliable but in old age can suffer from electrical gremlins – curable by re-wiring – and the thermostat may stop working, which increases fuel consumption. Experts, however, feel that injected cars run better than the carburettor models, and that the later injection systems are better than the earlier ones.

On the bodywork side, there are two very different stories to be told. The 120 series, while not totally immune to corrosion, is rarely badly affected by rust, but the 1800 rusts very badly indeed.

The 120 series was designed to survive the rigours of a Scandinavian – or North American – winter. This was reflected in the quality of the materials used, from the steel through extensive rust-proofing and the high quality paint finish, to exterior brightwork which was mostly anodised aluminium or stainless steel. In consequence it is now unusual to find a 120 series that requires major surgery. While there may be minor problems, they are usually easily spotted and fairly simple to deal with. Many original panels or repair sections are available, and prices are mostly very reasonable.

One persistent problem is that both windscreen and rear screen may leak, especially if replacement screens have been fitted incorrectly. At the front, such leaks can lead to severe corrosion in the front bulkhead structure and the footwells. While the one-piece rubber front floor mat helps to prevent the classic problem of dampness remaining in carpeting, water coming down the A-posts from above can eventually cause rust in the floorpan and chassis outriggers. At the front end of the car, mud thrown up by the front wheels can get trapped by the headlamp bowl or in the box section that runs along the top of the inner wing. Any corrosion in the inner wing structure will require new panels to be welded in. If the vertical seam between front wing and grille panel, running down from the headlamp, shows any sign of rust, the chances are that the inner wings are also beginning to corrode.

Any rust in the front lower crossmember of the body structure, behind the front bumper, is quite serious as the front anti-roll bar is attached to it. There is occasionally a problem with the front grille panel, particularly the structure behind the central divider: while there is a drainhole here, it can get blocked, allowing mud and

Although some of an 1800's sub-surface structure is shared with the 120 series, rectifying rust usually requires more extensive work.

water to build up with the inevitable result. The pointed centre of the grille panel may have become dented. It is unusual for the front suspension crossmember, which acts as a subframe for the engine, to be affected, and the front chassis legs also tend to survive very well, although they should be checked at the rear where they run into the main floorpan – rust here is potentially very serious.

The sills were galvanised from 1964. Their inner structure is usually very sound; if the outer sill panels have rusted, they are easily and cheaply replaced. The door bottoms may have rusted, again particularly if drainholes are blocked. New doors are not available but repair panels for the lower halves of the door skins, and for the bottom of the inner structure, are available. The double-skinned rear wheelarches suffer from internal condensation and this is one of the first areas where a 120 series may show signs of corrosion. Again, repair sections are available. The rear wings are not a problem, except for the lower fluted panels ahead of the rear bumper – and these are separate sections. Another weak spot is the rear reflector housings.

Inside the boot, the vulnerable areas are next to the wheelarches, with rust often triggered by water coming down from a leaking rear screen. The boot floor may rust through just behind the wheelarch, and corrosion can in bad cases begin to get into the chassis legs below the boot floor. The spare wheel well has a drainhole but if this gets blocked and water accumulates, sooner or later the inevitable result is a rusted-through spare wheel well. It should also be checked that the counter-balancing rods for the boot lid are working. The boot lid may corrode along its bottom edge, and on estate cars the lower

tailgate is similarly vulnerable. Another point to watch out for on an estate are the lower rear body sides, if dampness has penetrated the rubber seals of the long rear side windows.

Of the exterior brightwork, much is stainless steel or anodised aluminium, the major exception being the bumpers in high-quality chrome on quite thick steel. They do last a long time and can be replaced in sections – just as well as complete new bumpers are rather expensive. The interior, while somewhat spartan with vinyl trim and rubber floormats, is hard-wearing, although well-used front seats may be torn. Re-trimming can be difficult as most trim parts are not available. One particular problem is the black plastic covering above the dashboard which eventually begins to deteriorate from exposure to sunlight, and new covers are not available. The 120 series buyer is well advised to look for a car with as good an interior as possible.

Turning now to the 1800s, there are quite a few more rust problems. While 1800s of all ages can be affected, all cowhorn-bumpered cars sadly had particular problems because welding, sealing and build quality were frequently of a poor standard. A classic problem is that water comes down the A-post and enters the sill, which will then quietly rust through from the inside, eventually also spreading to the floorpan and the outriggers.

The front wings are vulnerable, and much more difficult – and expensive – to replace than 120 series wings because they are welded on. The front valance and the radiator crossmember may be affected, and the bonnet hinges, which are rather exposed at the front of the car, may seize solid. Although the suspension crossmember and the chassis legs are similar to the 120 series, they seem to rust more readily, and a particular problem is that the chassis leg may rust in the steering box area.

Rear wheelarches are also prone to rust, and water can get into the box section under the rear seats. On cars up to 1969 with the petrol filler flap next to the boot lid, the flap itself can rust if the drainhole is blocked. If water collects in the funnel around the filler, it can eventually penetrate the seal and seep down inside the filler neck, which will cause the petrol tank (which forms the boot floor) to rust through. Water may also collect in the channel around the boot lid aperture and eventually cause rust in the boot area generally, and the boot lid itself.

As many new panels or repair sections are now available for the 1800s as for the 120 series cars, but prices tend to be steeper. The interior causes a few problems of its own. Trim parts for the Jensen-built cars, many of

Build quality in latter years did not improve, so 1800ES models can rust **as badly as coupés. Despite their rarity, these cars are worth less.**

Still they are raced. Guido Enderle won his class in the 1995 German **historic saloon car championship with this wide-wheeled 123GT.**

which are unique, are difficult or impossible to find. The leather seats found on most cars may have worn or split, and retrimming will not be cheap. The floor carpets are inevitably not as hard-wearing as the rubber mats on the 120 series. Pre-1969 instruments with their rather fancy design are difficult to find. Clocks are reputed never to work properly and the tachometer tends to be famously inaccurate…

All in all, however, both the 120 series and the 1800 are unusually practical as classic cars. The 120 series cars are very suitable for everyday motoring, with good performance, excellent brakes and many worthwhile safety features. The original 1.6-litre models are now rare – there were not so many of them in the first place and they are particularly scarce in Britain. Most common in Britain is the 1.8-litre model, and most cars sold here were probably 122S twin-carburettor four-door saloons, often fitted with overdrive. One of these makes perhaps the most sensible 120 series for many enthusiasts. The estate car has its own following and is even more practical, especially if you need the extra carrying capacity; it is reputed to attract higher prices in the USA, if not in Europe. Greatly prized is the 123GT which is a genuine rarity.

The 1800s appeal to a rather different type of classic car enthusiast. They combine attractive looks – to most eyes anyway! – with a high level of practicality for anyone with no regular need to carry more than one passenger. In any case they are perhaps more likely to be kept as second cars. While the early Jensen-built cars are particularly sought-after, and while the 'cowhorn' front bumpers are a positive status symbol among 1800

aficionados, the mid-period 1800S models are reckoned to be the best blend of performance, practicality and simple maintenance. Unusual styling, relative rarity and added practicality are bonus points of the 1800ES, but this model rusts particularly badly and there are parts problems. Not surprisingly, 1800s of any kind command higher prices than 120 series cars.

Whichever is the Volvo of your choice, you will have a car which is pleasingly individualistic, long-lived and durable. They feel good to drive and betray their age mainly by the somewhat 'vintage' driving position, especially on the 1800, and the very period interior of the 120 series. The cars are well supported by enthusiastic clubs, and there are still so many parts available – not least from Volvo itself. But then this is what you would expect from a manufacturer which has built its reputation on the long life of its cars.

While these Volvos truly deserve their status as practical classics, there is another side to the 120 series and the 1800 – there is unquestionably a sporting feel to these cars. Epithets such as 'tractor' or 'tank-like' come too readily to mind when the talk turns to Volvos, but it is very unfair to judge these early cars by the yardstick one would apply to Volvos of the 1970s or 1980s. Those who are inclined to dismiss the 120 series or the 1800 simply because these are well-built, solid cars would do well to remember the vintage Bentley, which was famously dismissed by Ettore Bugatti, who said that he knew of no faster lorry. While the comparison between a vintage Bentley and a classic Volvo soon begins to falter, both breeds were endowed with that rare combination of sturdiness with sporting flair.

APPENDIX

Production figures ....

120 SERIES AND 1800 RANGE

As in most other Volvo publications, including official factory statistics, it has been assumed that all chassis numbers were issued and that production figures are therefore mostly identical with chassis number series. The main exception appears to concern 1969 model year 1800s, where eight chassis numbers appear not to have been issued. It is possible that not all overseas production (CKD assembly) is included. Production figures can only be split by body style, not by engine variations or by market.

Period	120 SERIES				1800 RANGE	
	Four-door	Two-door	Estate	Total	Coupé	1800ES
1956	249★★			249		
Jan 57 to Feb 58	4935			4935		
Feb 58 to Sep 58	6898			6898		
Sep 58 to Sep 59	15917			15917		
Sep 59 to Jul 60	26400			26400		
Aug 60 to Jul 61	29900			29900	500★	
Aug 61 to Jul 62	28500	10499	1399	40398	3500★	
Aug 62 to Jul 63	27200	29500	6875	63575	4000★	
Aug 63 to Jul 64	26400	44600	9675	80675	4499	
Aug 64 to Jul 65	27400	59800	11450	98650	4000	
Aug 65 to Jul 66	31250	72550	15200	119000	4500	
Aug 66 to Jul 67	9160	62950	17200	89310	4500	
Aug 67 to Jul 68		32600	8500	41100	2800	
Aug 68 to Jul 69		27500	2897	30397	1693	
Aug 69 to Jul 70		19919		19919	2799	
Aug 70 to Jul 71					4750	
Aug 71 to Jul 72					1865	3069
Aug 72 to Jul 73						5008
Totals	**234209**	**359918**	**73196**	**667323**	**39406**	**8077**

★Estimated splits between model years ★★ Pre-production models

No precise figure is available for the 123GT model; the best estimate is for the B18-engined model only, of around 1500 cars, of which 750 came in the 1967 model year and 750 in the 1968 model year.

Of the 120 series, 84,299 cars (all four-doors) had the B16 engine; 532,708 had the B18 engine (149,910 four-doors, 312,499 two-doors and 70,299 estates); and 50,316 had the B20 engine (47,419 two-doors and 2897 estates).

120 series: production of 667,323 between 1956-70.

1800 range: 47,483 coupés and estates built 1961-73.

Identification by chassis numbers ....

120 SERIES (AMAZON RANGE)

Each model is identified by a code number and a model year series letter. From September 1958 onwards, the first three figures of the code number are the model designation and decode as follows. First figure: 1 for saloon, 2 for estate. Second figure: 2 for four doors, 3 for two doors. Third figure: 1 for single carburettor engine, 2 for twin carburettor engine, 3 for GT-type engine. The fourth and fifth figures indicate the detailed specification, including the type of gearbox. The sixth figure or letter is 1 or V for left-hand drive, 2 or H for right-hand drive.

There are three different ranges of chassis numbers, one for each body style. The series letters and chassis number ranges by model year are quoted in the table below:

Period	Four-door: series letter, chassis number range		Two-door: series letter, chassis number range		Estate: series letter, chassis number range	
With B16 engine						
Oct 56 to Feb 58	A	1 to 5184				
Feb 58 to Sep 58	B	5185 to 12082				
Sep 58 to Sep 59	B	12083 to 27999				
Sep 59 to Jul 60	B	28000 to 54399				
Aug 60 to Jul 61	D	54400 to 84299				
With B18 engine						
Aug 61 to Jul 62	E	84300 to 112799	A	1 to 10499*	A	1 to 1399**
Aug 62 to Jul 63	F	112800 to 139999	B	10500 to 39999	B	1400 to 8274
Aug 63 to Jul 64	G	140000 to 166399	D	40000 to 84599	D	8275 to 17949
Aug 64 to Jul 65	K	166400 to 193799	E	84600 to 144399	E	17950 to 29399
Aug 65 to Jul 66	L	193800 to 225049	F	144400 to 216949	F	29400 to 44599
Aug 66 to Jul 67	M	225050 to 234209	M	216950 to 279899	M	44600 to 61799
Aug 67 to Jul 68			P	279900 to 312499	P	61800 to 70299
With B20 engine						
Aug 68 to Jul 69			S	312500 to 339999	S	70300 to 73196
Aug 69 to Jul 70			T	340000 to 359918		

* Two-door production began in Oct 61 ** Estate production began in Feb 62

1800 RANGE

As with the 120 series, each model year (or production period) is identified by a model year series letter. There are two different ranges of chassis numbers, one for all coupés (1961-72), the other for the 1800ES model (1971-73). The series letters and chassis number ranges by model year are quoted in the table below:

Period	1800 coupé: series letter, chassis number range		1800ES: series letter, chassis number range	
Built by Jensen (P1800 model)				
May 61 to Mar 63	A	1 to 6000		
Built by Volvo (1800S model)				
Apr 63 to Jul 63	B	6001 to 8000		
Aug 63 to Jul 64	D	8001 to 12499		
Aug 64 to Jul 65	E	12500 to 16499		
Aug 65 to Jul 66	F	16500 to 20999		
Aug 66 to Jul 67	M	21000 to 25499		
Aug 67 to Jul 68	P	25500 to 28299		
With B20 carburettor engine				
Aug 68 to Jul 69	S	28300 to 30000		
1800E fuel injection model				
Aug 69 to Jul 70	T	30001 to 32799		
Aug 70 to Jul 71	U	32800 to 37549		
Aug 71 to Jul 72	W	37550 to 39414	W	1 to 3069
Aug 72 to Jul 73			Y	3070 to 8077

Technical specifications.....................

120 SERIES, B16A engine, 121 saloon (1956-61)

Engine In-line four-cylinder **Construction** Cast-iron block and head **Crankshaft** Three main bearings **Bore × stroke** 79.37mm × 80mm (3.125in × 3.150in) **Capacity** 1583cc (96.6cu in) **Valves** Overhead valves operated by push-rods **Compression ratio** 7.4:1 **Fuel system** One Zenith 34VN carburettor **Maximum power** 66bhp at 4500rpm **Maximum torque** 85.3lb ft (11.8mkg) at 2500rpm **Transmission** Three-speed manual gearbox, synchromesh on second and third, all-synchro 'box 1960-61, overdrive optional 1960-61; four-speed all-synchro 'box optional from 1958; automatic clutch optional 1961; floor change, column change optional on four-speed export models 1961 **Final drive ratio** 4.56:1 **Top gear mph per 1000rpm** 15.9mph (26.6kph) **Brakes** Lockheed hydraulic, drum brakes front and rear, mechanical handbrake on rear wheels **Front suspension** Independent with wishbones and coil springs, telescopic shock absorbers, anti-roll bar **Rear suspension** Live axle, coil springs, torque arms and Panhard rod, telescopic shock absorbers **Steering** Cam and roller **Wheels/tyres** Steel disc wheels with 5.90-15 tubeless whitewall tyres **Length** 175.2in (4450mm) **Wheelbase** 102.4in (2600mm) **Width** 63.8in (1620mm) **Height** 59.25in (1505mm) **Front track** 51.8in (1315mm) **Rear track** 51.8in (1315mm) **Unladen weight** 2400lb (1090kg) **Gross vehicle weight** 3249lb (1475kg) **Top speed** 87mph (140kph) **0-60mph** est. 21sec **Standing ¼-mile** est. 25sec **Typical fuel consumption** 28mpg (10 L/100km)

120 SERIES, B16B engine, 122S saloon (1958-61)

As 121 saloon except: **Compression ratio** 8.2:1 **Fuel system** Two SU H4 carburettors **Maximum power** 85bhp at 5500rpm **Maximum torque** 86.8lb ft (12mkg) at 3000rpm **Transmission** Four-speed gearbox standard, except in Scandinavia **Top speed** 89-94mph (144-151kph) **0-60mph** 14-17sec **Standing ¼-mile** 19-21sec **Typical fuel consumption** 26mpg (11 L/100km)

120 SERIES, B18A engine, 121/131/221 models (1961-68)

Engine In-line four-cylinder **Construction** Cast-iron block and head **Crankshaft** Five main bearings **Bore × stroke** 84.14mm × 80mm (3.313in × 3.150in) **Capacity** 1780cc (108.62cu in) **Valves** Overhead valves operated by push-rods **Compression ratio** 8.5:1 (1961-65), 8.7:1 (1965-68) **Fuel system** One Zenith 36VN carburettor (1961-65), one Zenith-Stromberg 175CD or 175CDS carburettor (1965-68) **Maximum power** 75bhp at 4500rpm (1961-66), 85bhp at 5000rpm (1966-68) **Maximum torque** 101.3lb ft (14mkg) at 2800rpm (1961-66), 108.5lb ft (15mkg) at 3000rpm (1966-68) **Transmission** Four-speed all-synchro gearbox; three-speed 'box only available in Scandinavia 1961-62, and on 'Favorit' model 1965-68; Borg-Warner 35 three-speed automatic optional 1964-67 **Final drive ratio** Saloons 4.1:1, estate 4.56:1 **Top gear mph per 1000rpm** Saloons 17.8mph

(28.6kph), estate 17mph (27.3kph) **Brakes** Hydraulic drum brakes front and rear (1961-64); Girling disc brakes on front wheels, drum brakes on rear wheels (1964-68); servo standard on estate from 1964, on saloons from 1965; mechanical handbrake on rear wheels **Front suspension** Independent with wishbones and coil springs, telescopic shock absorbers, anti-roll bar **Rear suspension** Live axle, coil springs, torque arms and Panhard rod, telescopic shock absorbers; estate car: heavy-duty rear springs and rubber auxiliary springs **Steering** Cam and roller **Wheels/tyres** Steel disc wheels; tyre sizes: saloons: 5.90-15 (1961-63), 6.00-15 (1963-65), 165-15 (1965-68); estate: 6.40-15 **Length** Saloons 175.2in (4450mm), estate 176.8in (4490mm) **Wheelbase** 102.4in (2600mm) **Width** 63.8in (1620mm) **Height** Saloons 59.25in (1505mm), estate 60.25in (1530mm) **Front track** 51.8in (1315mm) **Rear track** 51.8in (1315mm) **Unladen weight** Two-door saloon 2357lb (1070kg), four-door saloon 2400lb (1090kg), estate 2621lb (1190kg); for models with automatic gearbox add approx. 110lb (50kg) **Gross vehicle weight** Saloons 3415lb (1550kg), estate 3877lb (1760kg) **Top speed** 87-91mph (140-146kph) **0-60mph** 16.6-21sec **Standing ¼-mile** 20.7-22 sec **Typical fuel consumption** 24-30mpg (11.9-9.5 L/100km)

120 SERIES, B18D engine, 122/132/222 models (1961-68)

As 121/131/221 models except: **Compression ratio** 1968 models: 10.1:1 **Fuel system** Two SU HS6 carburettors **Maximum power** 90bhp at 5000rpm (1961-65), 95bhp at 5400rpm (1966 models), 100bhp at 5700rpm (1967 models), 115bhp at 6000rpm (1968 models) **Maximum torque** 104.9lb ft (14.5mkg) at 3500rpm (1961-65), 107.1lb ft (14.8mkg) at 3500rpm (1966 models), 108.5lb ft (15mkg) at 3500rpm (1967 models), 112.2lb ft (15.5mkg) at 4000rpm (1968 models) **Transmission** Overdrive optional with four-speed 'box 1961-66; automatic optional only in North America 1964-66, in all markets 1966-67 **Final drive ratio** 4.56:1 on saloons with overdrive **Brakes** Girling front disc brakes from 1961, servo standard from 1964 **Unladen weight** For models with overdrive, add approx. 44lb (20kg) **Top speed** 94-97mph (151-156kph) **0-60mph** 13-15sec **Standing ¼-mile** 19-20sec **Typical fuel consumption** 23-32mpg (12.4-8.9 L/100km)

120 SERIES, B18B engine, 123GT two-door saloon (1966-68)

As 122/132/222 models except: **Compression ratio** 10.1:1 **Maximum power** 115bhp at 6000rpm **Maximum torque** 112.2lb ft (15.5mkg) at 4000rpm **Transmission** Overdrive standard **Final drive ratio** 4.56:1 **Top gear mph per 1000rpm** 15.8mph (25.5kph) **Wheels/tyres** Tyres 165SR-15 **Top speed** 102-104mph (164-167kph) **0-60mph** 11-13sec **Standing ¼-mile** 18-19sec **Typical fuel consumption** 22-23mpg (13-12.4 L/100km) (NB: the B18B engine was also fitted to certain other models, including some South African 1967 models, and effectively to 1968 models of the 132/222 range)

120 SERIES, B20A engine, '121' models (131 two-door, 221 estate) (1968-70)

As models with B18A engine except: **Bore × stroke** 88.9mm × 80mm (3.5in × 3.150in) **Capacity** 1986cc (121.19cu in) **Compression ratio** 8.7:1 **Fuel system** One Zenith-Stromberg 175 CD-25 carburettor

Maximum power 90bhp at 4800rpm Maximum torque 119.4lb ft (16.5mkg) at 3000rpm Transmission Four-speed manual all-synchro gearbox only Final drive ratio Saloon 4.1:1, estate 4.3:1 Top gear mph per 1000rpm 18mph (29kph) Brakes Now with dual circuit hydraulics Top speed est. 93-96mph (150-155kph) (NB: Estate car discontinued in May 1969)

120 SERIES, B20B engine, '122S' two-door saloon, 123GT (1968–70)
As models with B20A engine except: Compression ratio 9.5:1 Fuel system Two SU HS6 carburettors Maximum power 118bhp at 5800rpm Maximum torque 123lb ft (17mkg) at 3500rpm Transmission Overdrive fitted on 123GT model Final drive ratio 4.3:1 on 123GT model Top gear mph per 1000rpm 16.8mph (27kph) Top speed est. 102-106mph (165-170kph) (NB: 123GT model discontinued in 1969)

P1800/1800S COUPÉ, B18B engine (1961–68)
Engine In-line four-cylinder Construction Cast-iron block and head Crankshaft Five main bearings Bore × stroke 84.14mm × 80mm (3.313in × 3.150in) Capacity 1780cc (108.62cu in) Valves Overhead valves operated by push-rods Compression ratio 9.5:1 (1961–63), 10:1 (1963–68) Fuel system Two SU HS6 carburettors Maximum power 100bhp at 5500rpm (1961–63), 108bhp at 5800rpm (1963–65), 115bhp at 6000rpm (1965–68) Maximum torque 110lb ft (15.2mkg) at 3800rpm (1961–63) or at 4000rpm (1963–65), 112.2lb ft (15.5mkg) at 4000rpm (1965–68) Transmission Four-speed manual all-synchro 'box with remote-control floor change; overdrive optional (1961–63), overdrive standard (1963–68) Final drive ratio 4.1:1 (without overdrive), 4.56:1 (with overdrive) Top gear mph per 1000rpm 15.8mph (25.5kph) Brakes Girling hydraulic with servo, disc brakes front, drum brakes rear; mechanical handbrake on rear wheels Front suspension Independent with wishbones and coil springs, telescopic shock absorbers, anti-roll bar Rear suspension Live axle, coil springs, torque arms and Panhard rod, telescopic shock absorbers Steering Cam and roller Wheels/tyres Steel disc wheels with 165SR-15 Pirelli Cinturato tyres Length 173.2in (4400mm) (1961–64), 171.2in (4350mm) (1964–68) Wheelbase 96.5in (2450mm) Width 66.9in (1700mm) Height 50.6in (1285mm) Front track 51.8in (1315mm) Rear track 51.8in (1315mm) Unladen weight 2400lb (1090kg) Gross vehicle weight 3194lb (1450kg) Top speed 105-110mph (169-177kph) 0-60mph 12-14sec Standing ¼-mile 18-21sec Typical fuel consumption 23-27mpg (12.4-10.5 L/100km)

1800S COUPÉ, B20B engine (1968–69)
As model with B18B engine except: Bore × stroke 88.9mm × 80mm (3.5in × 3.150in) Capacity 1986cc (121.19cu in) Compression ratio 9.5:1 Fuel system Two Zenith-Stromberg carburettors Maximum power 118bhp at 5800rpm Maximum torque 123lb ft (17mkg) at 3500rpm Final drive ratio 4.3:1 Top gear mph per 1000rpm 16.8mph (27.1kph) Brakes Now with dual circuit hydraulics Unladen weight 2423lb (1100kg) Top speed est. 108-112mph (174-180kph)

1800E COUPÉ, B20E engine (1969–72); B20F engine (for North America 1971–72)
As model with B20B engine except: Compression ratio 10.5:1 (B20E), 8.7:1 (B20F) Fuel system Bosch electronic fuel injection Maximum power 130bhp at 6000rpm (B20E, 1969–71), 135bhp at 6000rpm (B20E, 1971–72), 125bhp at 6000rpm (B20F) Maximum torque 130.2lb ft (18mkg) at 3500rpm (B20E), 123lb ft (17mkg) at 3500rpm Transmission Borg-Warner 35 three-speed automatic optional 1970–72 Final drive ratio 3.91:1 on cars with automatic Brakes Discs also on rear wheels Wheels/tyres Cast aluminium wheels with steel rims (1969–71), pressed steel disc wheels (1971–72); 185/70HR-15 tyres (1971–72) Unladen weight 2533lb (1150kg) Top speed 108-112mph (174-180kph) 0-60mph 9-10sec Standing ¼-mile 17sec Typical fuel consumption 22-26mpg (13-11 L/100km)

1800ES SPORTS ESTATE, B20E/B20F engine (1971–73)
As 1800E 1972 model except: Maximum power 112bhp on North American 1973 models Length 172.6in (4385mm) Unladen weight 2621lb (1190kg) Gross vehicle weight 3304lb (1500kg) Top speed 110-112mph (177-180kph) Typical fuel consumption 21-26mpg (14-11 L/100km)

NOTES All technical specifications are based partly on Volvo's own literature and partly on the annual catalogue issue of *Automobil Revue* (Bern, Switzerland). All engine power and torque figures are SAE ratings as quoted by Volvo at the time of manufacture. Performance figures are from a variety of sources, including *The Autocar/Autocar, Autosport, The Motor/Motor, Motor Sport* (all in the UK), *Car and Driver, Road & Track* (both in the US) and other contemporary magazines. All fuel consumption figures in mpg are calculated per *imperial* gallon.

ACKNOWLEDGEMENTS

Grateful thanks are due to the owners whose cars were used for special photography by Tony Baker (in the UK) and Dieter Rebmann (in Germany): Edgar Blepp (1959 Amazon B16 and 1972 P1800ES), Julian Greenwood (1962 P1800), Barbara Morris (1965 P1800S and 1971 P1800E) and Kuno Haggenmiller (1966 Amazon estate and 1969 123GT). Photographic guidance was provided by John Smith and Nigel Keene of the Volvo Owners Club, and Notker Hibrenner of Volvo-Club e.V Deutschland. Advice for the P1800 sections, and a few photos, came from Kevin Price of the Volvo Enthusiasts Club. Archive photos came from Volvo Art Service (thanks to Carina Möller and Lisa Andersson), *Classic Cars* magazine (thanks to Maurice Rowe, Richard Eccleston, Liz Turner and Scilla Robinson), *Classic and Sportscar* magazine (thanks to John Blundell and Ed Herridge), Dieter Günther, Hannu Mikkola, Joginder Singh and Ole Sommer. Thanks also to Aubrey Brett.